372.5 FEH

REAL-WORLD READINGS IN ART EDUCATION

1801190.

This book is due for return on or before the last date shown below.

Don Gresswell Ltd., London, N21 Cat. No. 1208
DG 02242/71

REAL-WORLD READINGS IN ART EDUCATION

THINGS YOUR PROFESSOR NEVER TOLD YOU

edited by

DENNIS FEHR, KRIS FEHR,
AND KAREN KEIFER-BOYD

FALMER PRESS
A MEMBER OF THE TAYLOR & FRANCIS GROUP
NEW YORK AND LONDON
2000

Published in 2000 by
Falmer Press
A member of the Taylor & Francis Group
19 Union Square West
New York, NY 10003

10 9 8 7 6 5 4 3 2 1

Library of Congress Cataloging-in-Publication Data is available from the
Library of Congress.

Printed on acid-free, 250-year-life paper
Manufactured in the United States of America

We dedicate this book to art teachers, who empower their students to create and interpret an image-filled world; to art education majors, who have chosen one of humanity's most worthy endeavors; and to art students, who must challenge the aesthetic discourses that infuse their lives.

Contents

Part II
Real-World Aesthetics: Breaking the Rules 35
Kris Fehr

Part III
Real-World Art Lessons: Ignoring the Rules 73
Kris Fehr

Part IV
Real-World Structural Change: Rewriting the Rules 123
    Karen Keifer-Boyd

Acknowledgments

We thank Melody Weiler, Art Department Chair at Texas Tech University, for bringing together an art education faculty who share a vision of radical social change in which all people are responsible and free. We also thank our teachers and students (in the case of this book, especially five Texan art teachers: Helen Taylor, Anne Jones, Tiffanie Davis, Mary Lambeth, and Kathy Stout) for encouraging us to create a more humane world by reflecting on our teaching and teaching on our reflections.

Karen Kiefer-Boyd designed the cover. We thank Janna and Josh Toby for lending stuffed gorillas as a reference to Chapter 15, *A Field Guide for Art Educators: Guerilla Tactics for Change*. We also thank Future Akins for her class in which Karen made the spirit doll (see Chapter 12, *Simply Sacred*). We especially thank Mario Chagolla for allowing Karen to photograph the hood of his Lowrider and permitting us to use the photograph as a reference to Chapter 5, *Gender Politics in the Back Seat of a Lowrider*.

Introduction: Teaching as Transgression

DENNIS EARL FEHR

The question is this: What's missing from all that preening and horn blowing by the teachers-as-artists and the discipline-based art eddies? You're holding a book in which prominent critical art educators give some in-your-face answers, but first let's look at the horn blowing. The teacher-as-artist model—art ed as a series of studio activities with minimal linkage to art viewing or societal issues—dominated art education in the postwar 1940s and 1950s, boosted by Viktor Lowenfeld's *Creative and Mental Growth* (1947). Criticism of this model—in fact, the sprout that would grow into discipline-based art education (DBAE)—quickly emerged. In the 1960s Elliot Eisner (cf. 1972) and others, driven by a blend of noble intent and Getty Center money, tinkered with the idea that art ed could be defined as a series of disciplines. Their tinkering crystallized into DBAE in the 1980s.

Discipline-based art ed, popular though it is, has not replaced the artist-as-teacher model. Its staying power is suggested in the fall 1998 issue of *Studies in Art Education,* where we read that domination of Canadian and U.S. graduate art ed programs is shared by both approaches (Anderson, Eisner, & McRorie). And *Creative and Mental Growth* still sells so well that no one can keep track of which edition is current.

The irony of the teacher-as-artist model is that its proclaimed strength—studio production with little exposure to art exemplars or life outside the school—is its greatest weakness. First, this approach perpetuates the cocoonlike isolation from society that has served the art world so poorly in the twentieth century. By ignoring much of the content of visual art, this approach assures the subject's frill status in schools and undermines art's potential as an agent of social reconstruction.

Second, requiring children to make one artwork after another over the course of a school year without comprehensive study of strong work done by others is unfair. Why are our own studio walls covered with postcards of artists' openings and pages torn from *ArtFORUM*? Because we choose not to work in a vacuum. Because we are inspired by the work of others. Because we cannot individually generate many of the universal symbols found in our world's art heritage. How can we place studio demands on our students while denying them access to the symbology we provide ourselves? Such matters are part of what art educator Ed Check (personal communication, April 18, 1998) referred to when he said art education can be a silly field.

Even cynical postmodernists like me concede that in one way DBAE has benefited art education—it has made art viewing more important. Its problem is how it does this: DBAE is tainted with one of humanity's most enduring traditions—racism.

DBAE's roots reach back to ancient Greek philosophy (aesthetics), nineteenth-century U.S. academe (art history), and capitalist economics (criticism). Aesthetic philosophy is an ancient Western discipline, traceable at least to Plato. Greece was the cradle of Western civilization, and our students almost always study only Western—and for that matter, male—aestheticians.

What do Asian, African, Native American, and other cultures say about the nature of visual imagery? What have women, Western or non-Western, said? We don't know. And if we seek to answer these questions using DBAE, we must assume that DBAE's disciplines are applicable to these groups. This assumption is academically reckless and culturally arrogant. The answers are more honestly found by skipping DBAE and approaching our research with open minds and a cautious awareness of our Western biases (Fehr, 1995a).

A second DBAE discipline, art history, emerged in U.S. universities in the late nineteenth century. One of its goals was to create cultural parity with Europe's educated class. One of its results was to create a European canon, a standard by which to judge non-European art—that is, the remaining 95 or so percent of the world's art.

The same urge, this time couched in economic terms, drove the creation of the quintessentially Western field of art criticism. Art criticism has always been more an economic than an academic endeavor. Its primary purpose is to serve the *collectigentsia*'s practice of investing in art they don't understand. Twin ironies undermine DBAE advocates' strident justifications of this Eurocentric, capitalistic approach to art view-ing—the Western art community is beginning to accept world art on equal footing, and American schools are filling with children of all ethnicities.

At the 1996 annual conference of the National Art Education Associa-tion, I encountered a typically pinched perspective from a DBAE apologist from Penn State University, one of the Getty's six funded centers. I asked her how Getty foot soldiers justify DBAE's bastardizing of non-Western imagery. She responded that the Getty is increasing its non-Western curric-ular materials. I kindly and gently suggested that increasing a bad thing won't make it better. The conversation ended there—I think she said Bar-bara Walters was waiting to interview her, or something.

At Texas's state art ed conference in 1997, a prominent foot soldier from the University of North Texas, another funded Getty center, gave this answer to the same query: "That's not a problem because DBAE can be anything you want." This argument denies that DBAE is a model with four specified disciplines. If DBAE practitioners do realize the racial bias of these disciplines and consequently teach outside them, then they are no longer practicing DBAE.

So where do we go? Critical theory's emphasis on challenging au-thority seems to be one signpost of tomorrow's art education. Postmod-ernism's dismissal of grand narratives seems to be another. Add feminist consciousness-raising and the political activism of a host of marginal-ized groups, and a picture begins to emerge. The roots of this approach are not new—an early progressive call for art education to link itself with the rest of the world came from John Dewey in 1916. Manuel Barkan, a Deweyan art educator, wrote in 1955 that the social environment is the best place for children to grow into responsible adults. In 1961 June King McFee, one of the few prominent female voices in art education at the time, revived progressive populism by calling for art education for op-pressed groups.

Such visionaries may emerge as the most influential shapers of art education in the twenty-first century. Today, however, their observations are largely unaddressed in the professional literature, pushed aside by DBAE discussions of postimpressionism and teacher-as-artist tips on how to paint on aluminum foil—in other words, what many of us were taught in college.

This state of affairs is driving growing numbers of scholars to create a new place for art ed. In 1980 art educator Vincent Lanier called for making our youth literate about visual documents that explore their so-cial oppression. Andreas Huyssen (1990) advises abandoning the dead end created when modernists separated politics from aesthetics. Elizabeth Garber (1992) calls for curriculum building blocks about issues, themes, and cultural phenomena rather than formal art vocabulary, art styles, and canonical exemplars.

Building on these ideas, Kris Fehr, Karen Keifer-Boyd, and I, along with our panel of thoughtful authors, describe our vision of this place in this book. We transgress the bounds of art educational prudence—you will find radical theory, unconventional formats, informal English, controversial research models, and that most despised element in the world of academic writing—humor. Our audience is classroom art teachers and teachers in training, the people we feel are—along with schoolchildren—the most important constituencies in our field.

We feel that art teachers must protest, break, ignore, or rewrite the rules that trap art at the curricular periphery. Hence, the transgressive art teaching we describe in *Real-World Readings in Art Education* consists of a four-pronged assault: "Real-World Classroom Voices: Protesting the Rules"; "Real-World Aesthetics: Breaking the Rules"; "Real-World Art Lessons: Ignoring the Rules"; and "Real-World Structural Change: Rewriting the Rules."

The authors in Part I, "Real-World Classroom Voices: Protesting the Rules," roll up their sleeves and grapple with the gritty realities of teaching art today. Seasoned educators offer strategies for improving our daily classroom experiences.

The authors in Part II, "Real-World Aesthetics: Breaking the Rules," violate a number of art education's sacred codes. They challenge definitions of art held dear by many members of our field. They define good art in ways that will appall many an art historian. And they frankly describe what our culturewide reverence for the European patriarchal canon has done to children.

Part III, "Real-World Art Lessons: Ignoring the Rules," gets at the heart of the matter—guiding teachers in how to ignore rules that keep children from becoming thoughtful cultural critics through art. Each chapter offers alternative content in practical terms.

The authors in Part IV, "Real-World Structural Change: Rewriting the Rules," describe ways to radicalize school policy, curricula, and instruction. These include shifting from linear, textbook-based learning to the nonlinear realm of cyberspace. Not all art teachers welcome this challenge. One recently told me that making art with computers diminishes the immediacy of the aesthetic moment by placing technological intercessories between artists and their work. I told her I could imagine the same criticism befalling the first artisan to make a line with a charred stick instead of a soot-covered finger: "Hey, Org—you diminish immediacy of aesthetic moment by placing technological intercessory between you and work. Stop it!"

To summarize, we are living through an important moment on the West's millennial clock, a moment rich with symbolic opportunity. Countless marginalized groups are finding their voices and creating new art forms that hybridize components of their heritages with the heritages of the mainstream West. These art forms often represent a third culture, made of their experiences in the cultural borderlands (Fehr, 1995b). These cultures and their art forms cannot be understood within teacher-as-artist programs that disdain viewing and ignore social issues. And they cannot be depicted fairly within the morally troubling strictures of DBAE. *Real-World Readings in Art Education* offers teachers a democratic alternative based on this assumption: If art teachers want to make the world better, we must do more than decorate it.

REFERENCES

Anderson, T., Eisner, E., & McRorie, S. (1998). A survey of graduate studies in art education. *Studies in Art Education, 40* (1), 8–25.

Barkan, M. (1955). *A foundation for art education.* New York: Ronald.

Dewey, J. (1916). *Democracy in education.* New York: Macmillan.

Eisner, E. (1972). *Educating artistic vision.* New York: Macmillan.

Fehr, D. (1995a). Context-based art education: A new model for a new era. Keynote address to Michigan Art Education Association Annual Conference. Dearborn, MI. Internet: www2.tltc.ttu.edu/Fehr/

———. (1995b). Interview on *Libri: The Radio Book Review.* WPSU radio, State College, PA (an affiliate of National Public Radio). Internet: www2.tltc.ttu.edu/Fehr/

Garber, E. (1992). Feminism, aesthetics, and art education. *Studies in Art Education, 33* (2), 210–225.

Huyssen, A. (1990). Mapping the postmodern. In L. J. Nicholson, ed., *Feminism/postmodernism* (pp. 234–277). New York: Routledge.

Lanier, V. (1980). Six items on the agenda for the eighties. *Art Education, 33* (1), 16–23.

Lowenfeld, V. (1947). *Creative and mental growth.* New York: Macmillan.

McFee, J. (1961). *Preparation for art.* Belmont, CA: Wadsworth.

Real-World Classroom Voices: Protesting the Rules

KAREN KEIFER-BOYD

School authorities often intend their rules to be unquestioned. Yet the authors in Part I protest the perceived rules of art teacher expectations and art content. Rules are unquestioned theories that guide practice. Theory underlies all teaching. Our beliefs about children, about what teaching means, and about what we teach encompass our teaching theory. Part I can help us reflect on our teaching theory and practice. It will help us protest the rules that impose teaching contexts.

Real-World Readings in Art Education begins with teachers' stories in Kathleen E. Connors's chapter, "Familiar Voices and the Need for Reform," that protest the rift between the theories that they learned and their lived experiences as teachers. These teachers protest the dangers that their students encounter daily. They protest the loss of art facilities, the need to hide gay identity, the horrors of children's home lives, and the heaviness of grief that envelops their daily experience of teaching art in today's public schools. Some decide to move on, others to passively accept the situation. Some choose to stay closeted for their safety and to protect their reputations as good art teachers. However, others, by joining forces, networking, and "visually listening," tell how they protest with proactive practices that have made a difference.

In Chapter 2, "Making a Difference," Elizabeth Manley Delacruz provides a glimpse into the professional life of an art teacher and reveals the difficulties in achieving professional satisfaction and self-worth. Delacruz's goal in this chapter is to inspire art educators with suggestions for renewing professional aspirations. She offers suggestions for self-efficacy based on her own and other art teachers' needs, successes, and failures.

In Chapter 3, "Feminist and Critical Pedagogies: Intersections and Divergences," Yvonne Gaudelius protests teaching in which patriarchal constructions of knowledge dominate teacher practice. She distinguishes between critical and feminist theories and argues that teaching that does not include feminist issues promotes gender terrorism. Feminist theory applied to art teaching derives knowledge from women's contemporary and historic perspectives and practices. Debate, argument, and authority, by contrast, are critical pedagogical devices that are at odds with feminist pedagogy.

Gaudelius describes how theory informs practice and practice informs theory. She defines *pedagogy* as theoretically informed practice, and *radical pedagogy* as understanding teaching as a cultural practice. She argues that teachers not only need to examine critically the formation of knowledge but also work toward social and political equality. Gaudelius's postmodern writing moves from personal to political and back to personal, depending on how we read her parallel monologues, which join theory and practice to reveal how gender politics defines power in art education.

In Chapter 4, "Deconstructing Media Images of Postmodern Childhood," Paul Duncum challenges the sentimental and manipulative adult views of childhood that the corporate world propagates. Media constructions of childhood innocence influence art educational theory and practice. Mass-marketed images of children such as Precious Moments, *Teletubbies,* and Beanie Babies ignore the real lives of children. Duncum describes Anne Geddes's photographs as one of the best-known examples of this genre. Duncum proposes art curricula that make teachers and children aware of these media fictions. He asks the reader to notice two alternative views of children: the aesthetic child and the all-knowing child. In place of a singular view of the innocent child, this postmodern perspective conceives of childhood as varied fragments in search of coexistence.

CHAPTER 1

Familiar Voices and the Need for Reform

KATHLEEN E. CONNORS

Each teacher's narrative related here expresses a sense of betrayal by the promises of their training programs and certification requirements. These teachers describe how the daily inequities and inadequacies of their schools make it difficult to do their jobs. Their training programs required competence in creating art with a variety of media, as well as theoretical knowledge of education, psychology, and art. They learned to write art curricula. They acquired comprehensive knowledge of the European art canon. They trusted that this training prepared them to give to their chosen field. They believed they would help their future students begin lifelong relationships with art and meaningful encounters with self. They believed this because their university diplomas and state teaching certificates tacitly promised that they would be able to practice what they had learned. They would have eager students, adequate facilities, appropriate equipment, sufficient supplies, and enthusiastic support from parents, administrators, and faculty. Then they discovered the reality.

Not all art teachers tell this story, but too many who have taught during the past fifty years offer their variations on a familiar theme. Our teachers prepared us to work in ideal climes, but we find ourselves working in schools with manifold flaws. Typically, it is not the professors who misled us. In fact, professors often arrange field-based "real-life" encounters that contrast with the idealistic purview of textbooks, planned curricula, and state and national tests.

. When I became interested in inner-city teaching in 1970, one of my professors arranged for me to visit a school in Boston's Chinatown. A high metal fence with barbed wire at the top surrounded the school. A guard admitted visitors. The interior of the school looked like an elementary school I attended in the late 1940s—bolted-down desks and a cursive alphabet above the chalkboard in each room. The Chinese students (many non-English-speaking) sat facing forward, silently listening to a teacher lecturing in English from behind his desk. All of the building's teachers were English-speaking Anglos. Most were near retirement. The curriculum offered no art courses. The school's first goal was to maintain order. At that time no college course or professional exam took into account such a setting.

In 1971 I began student teaching in a school in Newton, Massachusetts, considered one of the state's exemplars of educational excellence. I expected an outstanding art program. What I found was that my supervising teacher taught 850 students every other week, traveling to two different schools. One school had no art room. We taught art in the hallway. The other school's art room was in a dark basement in what was once a gymnasium. The few lights that worked were fifteen feet above our heads. A constant din emerged from a doorless kindergarten room adjacent to the "art room." Our room provided the only access to the cafeteria, so teachers and children continuously paraded through the art room. My supervising teacher said this would be her last year to put up with such nonsense. Soon she would be certified to teach third grade. She could then have a room of her own, teach art every day, and finally learn the names of all of her students. The fact that she wore black every day spoke volumes.

The narratives that follow offer a small sampling of innumerable such events in our field. Each illustrates the rift between teacher certification programs and what we encounter. I chose to write these vignettes in the first person to convey the personal impact the situations had on the teachers. In all cases the versions are not verbatim, and the names are fictitious.

FROM A FIRST-YEAR TEACHER

This teacher wrote her story in one of my graduate seminars.

I was a pregnant first-year teacher, traveling between two elementary schools and teaching from a cart in both. One school had three stories and no elevator. I had to move the cart up and down the stairs. As my pregnancy progressed, a janitor took pity on me and moved the cart for me. The classroom teachers were mostly indifferent to my situation. Some even criticized me in front of their classes as I struggled to arrive on time and full of enthusiasm. I was afraid I would lose my job if I complained. My first year was pure hell.

CULTURE SHOCK IN THE INNER CITY

This teacher also wrote her story in one of my graduate seminars.

There I was, a blonde, blue-eyed, midwestern Protestant who had never seen an African American in person. I was about to begin teaching in a school with a student population that was 80 percent African American, 19 percent Hispanic, and 1 percent white. This was my third year of teaching but my first in the inner city, where I had always wanted to work. The school was across the street from a government housing project notorious for drug trafficking and drive-by shootings. The project was home to most of my students. Furthermore, I had recently married and converted to Judaism. These two personal events, combined with my new job and the neighborhood it was in, created much inner turmoil.

On the second day of school, a neighborhood gang shot a seven-year-old student of mine in the legs. This child was an innocent victim of a neighborhood gang war. Others in the school considered this incident tragic but common. To me, however, it was incomprehensible. I couldn't sleep. I felt that I was a member of no culture, yet obligated to many. I had wanted to teach in the inner city, since I believed in the power of art education to help make a difference. Yet most of my colleagues were burned out. They advised me simply to keep order in my classes and do holiday art.

As I came to know my students, I became aware not only of their neediness but also of my own. Many came to school without breakfast. Few wore clothes adequate for the cold weather. Most were from single-parent families and were labeled at risk.

Realizing that my students could not learn art until their basic needs were fulfilled, I recruited some other faculty to help me find organizations to assist families with parenting skills, conflict resolution, self-esteem, diversity, and issues of race, gender, and class. Our efforts resulted in a breakfast program and after-school workshops for parents.

After weeks of agonizing over how to heal myself and become the art teacher I hoped to be, I persuaded some teachers to cooperate with me on an interdisciplinary project I named The Big Book. The students in the project would write and illustrate a book about themselves, their lives, their families, and their heritages. The book would be "published" and kept in our library. The pages would be twenty inches by thirty inches—the size of poster board—giving the children plenty of room to tell their stories. Students and teachers began to stay after school to work on the book. It became a focal point of joy in learning and tolerance.

The finished book was a hit. Students who had not been involved wanted to make a book of their own. The book was only the first of many positive changes that occurred over the next few years. When a "better" school offered me a teaching position, I found the decision difficult. If only my university art education training had prepared me for this!

FOR THE GOOD OF THE FEW

This teacher also wrote her story in one of my graduate seminars.

The school where I taught art for fifteen years was built at the turn of the twentieth century. It had high ceilings and great windows. My art room had no sink, but the natural light was perfect. I was content, knowing some teachers in our district traveled between schools and taught from carts. Also, my school was in a residential area with lower crime. "Count your blessings," I told myself.

We always lacked art supplies. We relied on creative recycling and donations. Nevertheless, our students loved art, and their work impressed our administration, faculty, and parents. We art teachers received frequent praise for our students' accomplishments, especially those of "difficult" students whose art experiences taught them to love learning. I received the Teacher of the Year award in the same year that I lost my art room to the special education program. My replacement room was half the size, in the basement, separated from other classrooms, and next to the gym. The sounds of bouncing basketballs and screaming kids accompanied my classes. I did, however, have a sink.

I taught in the basement for five years, after which I transferred to an urban middle school in the same district. Some of my middle school students had been my students in the elementary school. One of the most surprising things I discovered was that few of them remembered the skills I was sure they had learned. Some acted as if they had never studied art. Their work had lost the spontaneity of elementary school. Was this simply a developmental phenomenon? Had the constant din from the gymnasium affected their long-term memory? Was their forty-minute-a-week schedule inadequate? Perhaps the message that art is not important is stronger in middle school. I wish I knew the reasons.

THE CLOSET AND TEACHING ART

The author of this narrative told it to me directly.

I teach high school art and coordinate the talented and gifted program in a large midwestern city. The student population in my school is primarily African American. I am white, Jewish, and gay. Nearly everyone in my school knows I am Jewish. No one knows that I am gay. Teachers who come out of the closet in my district eventually leave because of homophobic and heterosexist prejudices. My district has seen repeated instances of gay bashing and one murder. This is not surprising given the ease with which students can obtain weapons. Deaths, both accidental and intentional, have occurred in the district because students brought firearms to school. Consequently, I choose to remain in the closet. I also believe that I could no longer be an effective teacher if students, faculty, and administration defined me as a queer instead of as an art teacher. Outside of my profession I am out of the closet, but I don't feel that the time is right to come out at work. I love teaching art, especially when I see it change my students' lives. I feel a sense of accomplishment when my students, talented or not, begin to see the world as a positive place. I wait for the day when it is positive enough for me to come out.

THE CHILD FIRST?

This narrative came from a teacher/graduate student who sought my advice on how to handle a case of child abuse.

I had been teaching elementary art for seven years when Joey arrived at our school. His mother's trial for murdering her husband and daughter and abusing Joey was about to begin, so Joey moved to the home of his aunt and grandmother. Joey was with his mother when the murders took place, but no one knew how much he had witnessed.

He entered my third-grade art room with a special education teacher. He was withdrawn and sullen. All I could think was, "I am not trained to deal with this child's problems," so I consulted with his special education teacher, his aunt, his grandmother, the school social worker, and a psychologist. They agreed that Joey needed one-on-one teaching. I arranged to have him come to the art room during my preparation times. Progress was minimal at first, but by the end of the school year, Joey was spontaneously trying new media, telling stories about his creations in two and three dimensions, and creating works that were strictly from his own growing visual literacy.

Suddenly, we heard that Joey was going to be transferred back to his mother. We were shocked to learn that she had been acquitted on a technicality and granted custody of Joey.

At first I felt helpless. I did not know if options existed for cases such as this. Then I decided to inform Joey's new art teacher of his history. I sent her copies of my records as well as all the art he had created. She phoned me and asked if we could maintain contact about Joey. I was relieved that his new school had such a caring individual. I still fear for Joey, but now he may not fall between the cracks of institutional neglect.

TWENTY-FIVE YEARS OF TEACHING AND STILL LEARNING

As I listened to this narrative, I felt as if I were present, observing the teacher and student, visualizing every detail of the incident. Consequently, I chose to tell it in the third person.

She was the sole art teacher in an urban elementary school. It was October, and most of her students were eager to express artistically their delight and fascination with Halloween, while others did not celebrate the holiday for religious reasons. The teacher's solution was to create a comprehensive lesson on things to celebrate about autumn. Not surprisingly, many students picked spooky themes about Halloween, its history, and its icons.

Clarissa, a fourth grader, silently drew a pastel image of a graveyard. She depicted four graves, but only three had headstones. The first inscription was "Daddy," the second "Uncle Joseph," and the third "Aunt Vera." The fourth was simply a grave mound covered with flowers. The image's content and Clarissa's demeanor concerned the art teacher. She asked Clarissa to stay after class. After the other students left, she gently asked Clarissa if she would like to talk about her picture. With tears in her eyes, Clarissa explained that the graves were for family members who had died of AIDS. The grave without a headstone was her mother's. The family could not afford another headstone.

Clarissa said she was glad she could talk about this and make a picture about it because until then no one had let her talk about her feelings. Until then, the art teacher had heard only that one of her fourth-grade students had AIDS but did not know which one. Clarissa did not appear to know. Now the art teacher could show the picture to the school psychologist. The art teacher said this incident deepened her belief in the power of art to express truth and enable people to share their humanity. Without this chance to express her grief, the child may not have received the attention she deserved. Art reminds us of the value, meaning, and purpose of life.

SUGGESTIONS—AT THE RISK OF OVERSTATING THE OBVIOUS

The accounts in this chapter attest to the extraordinary work art teachers do in hostile environments with limited resources. One can only imagine possible accomplishments if art education had as much support as teacher-training programs often imply that it has. How, then, should these programs prepare our teachers? How should we evaluate their worthiness?

A survey of our field's professional literature makes clear that these problems are not new, and neither are my suggestions, other than perhaps my insistence that we become proactive. In doing so, we must realize that change may be difficult, but it is possible.

To define art education realistically, we must first define ourselves. A reactive approach allows others to define us. Then we must narrow the gap between research and practice. Computer technology has created wider access to research findings, and these findings must be field tested.

One proactive approach is to use popular media and computer technology to teach society that art promotes high-order and critical thinking, social responsibility, and psychological health. Art teachers can seek funding for such campaigns from such entities as Disney and the Getty Foundation. We should have our achievements, contributions to American education, and goals as a subject on *Oprah*!

We should demand culturewide support for art education programs. From Walter Smith to discipline-based art education, we own a reactive history. Our field is too white, too female, and too middle class. University art education faculty can recruit more diverse student populations. All teacher education and educational administration students must be schooled in art education.

As long as we allow elementary art classes to last an hour or less per week, and in upper grades often not at all, and as long as we allow art education to occur in hallways, basements, and cafeterias, or on pushcarts, society's chances of becoming visually literate are nonexistent. Members of our profession with clear-eyed visions must educate others. Art must be central to elementary curricula if we are to meet the implications of our training courses and certification requirements.

Public education is wrapped within layers of socioeconomics and cultural politics. Art educators, rather than allowing ourselves to be marginalized, should be at the center of movements to make our schools safer, cleaner, and more innovative. Textbooks, university programs, and certification exams must include both the positive and negative realities of our field. Until they do, they will continue to mislead art education students and widen the rift between theory and practice.

CHAPTER 2

Making a Difference

ELIZABETH MANLEY DELACRUZ

Sheryl Smetana begins each morning by teaching elementary art in Barrington, Illinois. At noon, she drives to the middle school to teach art to gifted sixth, seventh, and eighth graders. She then travels back for three more elementary art classes in the afternoon. She eats lunch on the run. She has no time to use the restroom. She teaches some of her classes on the stage in the gymnasium. Sheryl has no common planning time with other teachers in her school, and the elementary art teachers in Sheryl's district report that the secondary art teachers are uninterested in meeting with them. Sheryl is fighting to keep her gifted program from being cut.

Yet Sheryl does find time to read extensively about art and teaching. After Sheryl became excited about a paper written by Christine Thompson and Sandra Bales (1991), for example, she instituted the use of sketchbooks in the kindergarten art lessons.

Two of the best-kept secrets in art teacher education are how hard our students will work as teachers and how poorly society will regard their efforts. Teachers enrolled in my off-campus graduate courses tell about life in the schools. They remark that parents, teachers, and administrators view their programs as unimportant.

Even undergraduate art education majors experience this undervaluing. They consistently report that peers and faculty in other programs— art majors and faculty in particular—view them as less talented, and non-art majors outside the college regard art education as a trivial profession. Awareness of the low regard of peers begins in college and continues throughout art teachers' careers.

Low regard by others, compounded by the complexities and frustrations of classroom life, take their toll on art teachers' feelings of self-worth. This, in turn, prevents teachers from reaching their aspirations and negatively affects their impact on students.

This chapter concerns the poor conditions faced by many art educators and how these conditions influence teachers' professional satisfaction and self-worth. Recognizing these conditions from several studies of teachers and classrooms led me to develop suggestions for maintaining and renewing professional aspirations.

But let's return to Sheryl for a moment. I once asked her, "What good is art education research to you?"

Sheryl replied, "It keeps me as an active learner. This kind of education is empowerment. It enhances my awareness of what's being done . . . and that I don't have to start from square one. It's like, yeah, I saw this all along in my classrooms, but now I have access to something more."

Sheryl strives to connect art education readings to her teaching, but she finds much of the literature inaccessible and remote. She is uninterested in rehashing what she calls "old issues about creativity, copying, or bizarre drawing experiments," and she becomes irritated, along with her teacher friends, when her reading assignments do not reflect the realities of classroom life in today's schools. "C'mon," she admonishes her friends in academia, "we're the ones that are out there . . . help us!"

HELP WANTED: RESPONSES

Help us! Sheryl's plea echoes my own from my days as an art teacher. Looking for advice about managing the classroom, developing good lessons, coping with an overwhelming schedule, and improving the low status of the art program in my community, I turned to my university mentors. In retrospect, I see my return to academic life as a way of renewing my commitment to professional growth.

Why did we choose this profession? Laura Chapman (1982) and Wanda May (1989) write about how it feels to be an art teacher in a system that places little value on the arts. Chapman believes art educators at all levels contribute to the problems of our profession. She points to a failure of leadership within professional organizations and at the university level, and she criticizes art teachers themselves for engaging in haphazard teaching that lacks a clear understanding of what knowledge and skills in the arts are worthwhile.

May identifies the following constraints on teachers' aspirations:

views of teaching as "noble" and therefore unrewarded by extrinsic means such as status and income; views of teaching as women's work; the isolating cellular structure of schools; teachers' invisible workloads; and the "de-skilling of teachers," wherein outside experts prescribe educational programs, and teachers execute prescribed reforms. She calls for a more supportive environment, in which teachers have time and resources to collaborate and deliberate.

But prescriptions for real reform, May (1989) argues, must address the constraints that define teachers' work in real classrooms—a tall order for a profession that supports little research about the workplace. Few research endeavors explore ways to help art teachers cope with the overwhelming demands of the workplace, why good art teachers burn out, or why they decide to leave teaching. May argues that university educators who do not address the difficulties of teaching perpetuate these conditions. She suggests that those who lead teacher certification programs engage in more participative work with public school teachers.

Researchers in other fields conduct much of the research on teacher thinking and classroom life in non-art classrooms, but a handful of studies of art teaching exist and reveal recurring themes. James Gray and Ron MacGregor observed that art teachers typically encounter within the same classroom both highly talented, self-directed students and students who are distractive and unproductive (Gray, 1992). Mary Stokrocki (1988, 1990a, 1990b) describes art teachers' reactions to the conditions of their work, particularly in relation to students' mood swings and disruptive behaviors in the classrooms and to their oppressive institutional conditions (i.e., large classes, inadequate funding, inferior supplies, and poor administrative support). Anne Bullock and Lynn Galbraith (1992) identify themes that illustrate the detrimental effects of the workplace—a sense of dissonance, frustration, urgency, and compromise—as art teachers learn to negotiate the realities of school life. I hesitate to paint such a picture for my undergraduate students aspiring to become art teachers.

PROFESSIONAL ASPIRATIONS AND TEACHERS' SELF-EFFICACY

Student attitudes, behaviors, and accomplishments influence how teachers feel about their professional lives. Conversely, teachers' perceptions and expectations shape student attitudes and academic success. In a multischool study of teachers, Patricia Ashton and Rodman Webb (1986) found that teacher self-efficacy, a belief in one's ability to successfully teach all students regardless of their ability levels or backgrounds, significantly affected student achievement. Student achievement, for both low-achieving and high-achieving students, was higher in the classes of high self-efficacy teachers and lower in the classes of low self-efficacy teachers. In classrooms with high self-efficacy teachers the following commonalties were identified: (1) students shared the teacher's goals for the class; (2) students shared the teacher's definitions of what it means to be a teacher and to be a student; (3) the students and the teacher were willing to help one another achieve the class objectives and to fulfill the responsibilities of their respective roles; and (4) both students and the teacher shared a sense of pride in what they had accomplished. High self-efficacy teachers greeted their students at the door and talked with them before class. When the bell rang, they got their students' attention and went directly to work. They kept all students on track throughout the lesson.

Teachers with low self-efficacy called on low-achieving students less often and seldom encouraged these students to do their work, do it well, and turn it in on time. Frequently the work assigned to these students appeared trivial, designed to keep them busy so the teacher could teach the "brighter ones." Some low self-efficacy teachers engaged in what Ashton and Webb (1986) term excommunication tactics, sending low achievers to the library or to another part of the room to do work without instruction. Students were well aware of these teachers' attitudes toward them from their negative comments. Ashton and Webb (1986) argue that when teachers stratify their classes according to ability and give preferential treatment (more instruction, more assignments, more appropriate praise and corrective feedback) to some while neglecting others, all students are likely to learn where they stand in the teacher's pecking order.

School Ethos

Ashton and Webb (1986) observe that a teacher's positive sense of self depends on school organization, leadership, and ethos—the school's distinguishing habits and customs. Poor working conditions or unhealthy school environments can wear down teachers' self-efficacy. In schools supporting high self-efficacy teachers, principals viewed teachers as coworkers, established open channels of communication, and deferred decision making to teachers whenever appropriate. Teaming, subject area departmentalization, and collegial relations also contributed to high teacher self-efficacy. Ashton and Webb (1986) conclude that the single most important element in fostering successful students is positive school ethos, the result of an accumulation of factors such as high expectations for student achievement from both teachers and administrative staff, clear incentive and reward systems, continual monitoring of student work, and a high regard and institutional support for teachers.

Unfortunately, workplace conditions often make it difficult for teachers to maintain a high sense of self-efficacy. Teacher stress, frustration, and disillusionment are our foremost occupational health hazards and are the natural response to an oppressive work environment. We also share a perplexing social reality, where teacher bashing is rampant. Teachers are held accountable for the most unreasonable expectations, the major one being that we can solve the ills of society by doing a better job or, even worse, by being smarter or working harder.

Stressful conditions unique to art teaching include uninterested students who are advised into our classes by guidance counselors who conclude those students "can't make it in the academic classes" (a common practice in the high schools referred to as dumping), budget and program cuts and the ever present threat of them, and knowledge that our work is not well regarded. I offer suggestions here for those asking the same kinds of questions that I have: How can I make my classes the kinds of places where students want to be? And how can I make my work more personally satisfying?

HOW TO COPE WITH ART-TEACHING CONDITIONS

Environmental conditions include quality of light and air, acoustics, white noise, intercom announcements, clutter, room temperature, and room cleanliness (Susi, 1989). In many cases we can adjust the organization and cleanliness of the room, lighting, temperature, and ventilation (Susi, 1989). When we cannot change environmental conditions, coping is an appropriate decisive action. Coping does not mean ignoring a problem; it means identifying that problem and learning how to live with it. Deliberative coping reduces anxiety.

The best strategy for minimizing student behavioral disruptions is to establish clearly defined procedures and expectations early in the school year. Consistent monitoring and classroom maintenance are also necessary. Some sources of teacher stress include what Robert Laslett and

Colin Smith (1984) call the student irritation factor, time-honored ploys that students have used to gain distraction from their work. Movement, especially with the more fluid group activities, is particularly problematic for art teachers. During such activities, students' temptation to chatter or wander off task is greater. Teachers may give credit to some students for skillful acting. When apprehended, these students often falsely claim to have been in search of materials or fascinated with the work of a classmate. The volume and relevance of what is said can easily become matters of contention between art teachers and students. Less-experienced teachers tend to overreact and respond too harshly. In sum, prevention, monitoring, and a sense of perspective reduce many of the minor stresses and potential conflicts in the classroom.

Keep a Journal to Discover and Change Patterns

Keeping an accurate written account, a teaching journal, of stressful situations or discipline problems illuminates hidden patterns of thought and interaction. I kept such a journal while teaching high school art. I focused my writing on a particular freshman student who frequently disrupted class. After school I wrote down everything I remembered each time a disruption occurred. After a few weeks of writing and reflecting, I was able to identify how I contributed to these disruptions. I had enabled the student to engage me in unproductive verbal entanglements with other students as an audience. The very next time the student initiated, I disengaged from my usual pattern of response, realizing that the show before peers was part of the strategy of this student. The disruptions ceased.

Build Partnerships

Building partnerships, by networking with trusted colleagues, is also helpful in dealing with workplace stress. Moral support among peers can be very uplifting. Art teachers are often their own worst enemies when it comes to building partnerships. We work in our rooms during lunch and planning periods (if we even have planning periods) and bury ourselves before and after school in our work. In so doing we eliminate our opportunity for professional contact with other teachers in our schools and further isolate our programs. It is hard to accept that it is not wasteful to spend time with other teachers in the hallways, in the teachers' lounge, and in the offices, and that time so spent can be as vital to our professional lives as managing material, erecting displays, or grading student artwork. In building professional friendships, it is critical to avoid the "burnouts" (teachers who have given up). Burned-out teachers know everything that is wrong with students, parents, other teachers, the administrators, the schools, and the community, but they have no solutions. Their pessimism and despair are depressing and infectious. Instead, find teachers who have learned how to motivate their students, and spend time with these teachers.

Adhere to a Practicality Ethic

Art teachers who observe advancements in the field are aware of the multitude of voices calling for them to make their programs more comprehensive, integrative, outcome based, multicultural, gender sensitive, environmentally aware, and technologically advanced (Mims & Lankford, 1994). Sandra Mims and Louis Lankford observed that all of these pressures contributed to myths of superarteducators. Overwhelmed by pressures to do everything, art teachers develop a sense of inadequacy, guilt, and frustration. Mims and Lankford recommend that art teachers, rather than attempting to follow every trend, simply make decisions based on their own circumstances and sense of rightness and commit themselves to a few attainable objectives each year.

Teachers should decide whether to incorporate new materials or approaches based on their knowledge of what works in their classroom and congruence with their teaching style and with the types of students in their program. William Doyle (1986) calls this a practicality ethic. By making practical short-range and long-range plans that incorporate incremental improvements each year, art teachers may gain that sense of pride that comes with professional growth and avoid the stress of trying to do too much or make major changes all at once (Mims & Lankford, 1994).

SUSTAINING PROFESSIONAL ASPIRATIONS

Stories of the failure of teachers, students, and schools have dominated popular and news media. Success stories, as few as they are, tell of teachers' extraordinary personal sacrifices and stamina in the face of overwhelming odds. The quiet, ordinary successes that occur in most classrooms with good teachers and students are not newsworthy. Despite the constant barrage of criticism, or the tales of superhero teachers and mythic classrooms, the best classrooms are those in which ordinary teachers and students, when they go home to their families, can say, "Today was a good day, and I look forward to tomorrow."

Long-term professional vitality for art teachers in the public schools requires learning how to sustain a sense of power—which means holding on to high expectations for students—amid the demands and conditions of the workplace. Professional growth involves participation in our professional associations, networking, reasonable goal setting within the contingencies of our own teaching situations, and reflection on our own practices and habits of thought. Professional integrity for university art educators includes participatory work with public school art teachers. Properly nurtured, our belief in our collective power to make a difference in the lives of students can last a lifetime.

REFERENCES

Ashton, P., & Webb, R. (1986). *Making a difference: Teachers' sense of efficacy and student achievement.* White Plains, NY: Longman.

Bullock, A., & Galbraith, L. (1992). Images of art teaching: Comparing the beliefs and practices of two secondary art teachers. *Studies in Art Education, 33* (2), 86–97.

Chapman, L. (1982). *Instant art, instant culture: The unspoken policy for American schools.* New York: Teachers College.

Doyle, W. (1986). Classroom organization and management. In M. Wittrock, ed., *Third handbook of research on teaching* (pp. 392–432). New York: Macmillan.

Gray, J. (1992). An art teacher is an art teacher is an art teacher . . . fortunately! *Art Education, 45* (4), 19–23.

Laslett, R., & Smith, C. (1984). *Effective classroom management: A teacher's guide.* New York: Nicolas.

May, W. (1989). Teachers, teaching and the workplace: Omissions in curriculum reform. *Studies in Art Education, 30* (3), 142–156.

Mims, S., & Lankford, E. (1994). The new art education and what we've learned from superwoman. *Art Education, 47* (3), 57–61.

Stokrocki, M. (1988). Teaching preadolescents during a nine-week sequence: The negotiator approach. *Studies in Art Education, 30* (1), 39–46.

———. (1990a). A cross-site analysis: Problems in teaching art to preadolescents. *Studies in Art Education, 31* (2), 106–117.

————. (1990b). Forms of instruction used by art teachers with preadolescents. In B. E. Little, ed., *Secondary art education: An anthology of issues* (pp. 35–46). Reston, VA: National Art Education Association.

Susi, F. (1989). The physical environment of art classrooms: A basis for effective discipline. *Art Education, 42* (4), 37–43.

Thompson, C., & Bales, S. (1991). Michael doesn't like my dinosaurs. *Studies in Art Education, 31* (1), 43–51.

CHAPTER 3

Feminist and Critical Pedagogies: Intersections and Divergences

YVONNE GAUDELIUS

What is pedagogy? This question poses a good beginning for discussing radical pedagogies. I encourage you to stop reading for a moment. Close your eyes and answer the question. Perhaps a particular teacher comes to mind. Or a particular course. Or something you once read. Visualize your own experiences as you consider your definition of *radical pedagogy*. What images does this term conjure?

However you have answered these questions, keep your thoughts floating in your mind as you read the rest of this chapter. My intention is that you move in and out of your reading to encounter, remember, question, and theorize about what radical pedagogy means to you and that you make it a cornerstone of your teaching.

PEDAGOGY EXPLORED

One response to the question is that pedagogy refers to teaching. Some might connect it only to teaching methods. Others might feel that pedagogy refers to everything a teacher does.

Perhaps the most useful definition of pedagogy is more complex, however. Educator Jeanne Brady (1995) offers this observation:

I clearly remember reading Julia Kristeva's *Stabat Mater* (1977) for the first time. At certain points the text is split into two columns. In one column Kristeva wrote of women's experiences with semiotic and prelanguage as it relates to pleasure, or *jouissance*. She discussed the lack of discourse on maternal perspectives. In the

Pedagogy . . . means much more than simply "teaching." Pedagogy is more complex and encompassing. . . . Pedagogy does not address [only] methodology . . . in the form of "what works" but rather situates practice within a realm of cultural politics. (p. 7)

other column she wrote of birthing and mothering her son. Kristeva's splitting of her text, a seeming disjunction, transcended boundaries imposed by traditional academic discourse and paradoxically made the writing more whole.

Pedagogy does address the methodology of classroom practice; however, it is not limited to tips-'n'-tricks formulae. In the most meaningful sense, pedagogy includes not only everything that happens in schools but also an awareness that school events are bound within myriad institutional and cultural influences outside the schools.

David Lusted (1986) offers this definition:

[Pedagogy] draws attention to the *process* through which knowledge is produced. Pedagogy addresses the "how" questions involved not only in the transmission or reproduction of knowledge but also in its production. Indeed, it enables us to question the validity of separating these activities. . . . How one teaches is therefore of central interest but, through the prism of pedagogy, it becomes inseparable from what is being taught and, crucially, how one learns. (p. 3)

Framed in this way, pedagogy is located within a larger institutional and cultural sphere. Lusted adds that pedagogy does not exist as a separate entity for teacher and student, but rather that both teach and learn—in our case, about art. This definition suggests that pedagogy includes issues of both form and content, and that its forms may change depending upon practitioners' beliefs about knowledge.

Lusted suggests that pedagogy consists of three "agencies—the teacher, the learner and the knowledge they together produce" (p. 3). I add a fourth—the larger cultural and institutional sphere within which schools function. This addition points out that knowledge constructed within the school is inseparable from knowledge constructed outside the school. For example, our students learn about visual imagery through popular culture as readily as they learn about it in the art classroom.

Some define radical pedagogy as teaching practice viewed as cultural practice. Two common types of radical pedagogy are feminist pedagogy and critical pedagogy. In the next section of this chapter, I discuss what these two approaches offer art educators.

FEMINIST PEDAGOGY AND CRITICAL PEDAGOGY

Both feminist and critical pedagogies position teaching as cultural practice. Both approaches consider the impact of formal education on society. Educational historians trace each to the 1960s (although different impetuses fueled each).[1] Both guide students to examine the processes through which society creates knowledge. Both enable students to contribute to knowledge production. Finally, although these two forms of pedagogy question authority in different ways, empowerment is the goal of both.

I practice what I call feminist pedagogy. When I first began, I intended to use it to "change the world." I believed I could use feminist pedagogy to teach any subject to any group of students. I soon realized, however, that feminist pedagogy was not applicable to every situation or for every teacher. One important way that this realization came about was through conversation with other teachers. They would ask me questions such as How is feminist pedagogy different from good teaching? Initially I replied that feminist pedagogy emphasizes students' empower-

In this section I explore my experiences as a teacher. I do not intend this textual structure as a split between theory and practice or as a split between the academic and the personal. Rather, it is a way of using differing modes of discourse to discuss a set of ideas.

I have chosen this structure to engage in one of the most important aspects of radical pedagogy: self-reflection. I offer my reflections as starting points for others to begin their own pedagogical reflections.

These two forms of pedagogy differ mostly in theory. Feminist pedagogy is directly connected to feminist theory, while critical theory is rooted in the Frankfurt School (an early-twentieth-century group of European intellectuals) and the work of Brazilian educator Paulo Freire.

In *Pedagogy of the Oppressed* (1990), Freire defined pedagogy as liberatory teaching with a goal of social equality. He rejected the banking concept of education—students as receptacles and teachers as bankers, depositing information for student retrieval. Instead, Freire argued, "liberating

ment through finding their
voices and creating knowledge.
As I heard myself speak, I realized that, to my colleagues, I
was simply describing good
teaching.

education consists in acts of cognition, not transferals of information" (p. 67). Freire points out that
what is liberatory cannot be imposed, but rather emerges from
various settings and groups and
hence may take various forms.

I also realized that the kind of teaching my colleagues considered good may not include feminist concerns of gender, identity, and equality, although feminists had been instrumental in changing education.

I came to understand that feminist pedagogy and "good teaching" share many methodological features, but they may differ in content. If skillful teachers teach only from a patriarchal perspective, they limit students to a singular view. For example, art history course participants allowed an equal voice still cannot consider alternative perspectives if they view and read only work by white males.

Feminist pedagogy does not isolate the classroom from its cultural setting. Feminist educational theorists have examined how power is gendered in such settings (Lewis, 1992; Walkerdine, 1992; Weiler, 1988). I have learned from my own teaching in a large university that the classroom is not a neutral place. Before my students and I meet for the first time, we have determined our pedagogical expectations in gendered ways. Two distinct groups of students demonstrated this in their differing responses toward my inclusion of feminist material. When I teach women's studies classes, my students expect the course to focus on feminist issues (even though they might resist and challenge the ideas that are being presented). In the art education classroom, students occasionally challenge the inclusion of feminism. Some suggest that I am not offering a fair representation of what they need to know and that my personal agenda supersedes their needs.

An important critical theorist, Henry Giroux (1991),[2] defines pedagogy as transformation and teachers as forces behind this transformation. He stresses that teaching is more intellectual than

Expectations for information delivery exist beyond any particular classroom. Despite my encouragement to voice their ideas and take ownership of the material they study, many of my methodological. Unfortunately, his work lacks descriptions of specific teaching practices. Giroux (1991) defines pedagogy as a vehicle for theorizing about teaching rather than an activity that occurs in classrooms. His approach comes from a cautionary desire to avoid giving teachers "methodologies" that they then might adopt in cookie-cutter fashion. Giroux (1991) argues that teachers must apply critical pedagogy thoughtfully according to their specific classroom settings.

Giroux's work might be more useful if he discussed his own teaching practice while refraining from universalizing critical pedagogy (Gore, 1993). Homa Hoodfar (1997) suggests that proponents of critical pedagogy *theoretically* recognize that subject position matters, but that this attention to race, sex, gender, and sexuality has not carried over into how critical pedagogy *practices*. She adds that techniques to be used to challenge the status quo are not themselves appreciated as gendered and racialized (p. 211).

students believe or pretend to believe that I, the teacher, have the "right" answers. This makes my liberatory pedagogy difficult. I may have studied much that my students are only beginning to consider, and perhaps they should know much that I know, but perhaps some of it they do not need to know. Therefore what matters is that they acquire not a wealth of knowledge, but rather the ability to develop theory. I want my students to be able to discuss the main points of, say, Judith Butler's arguments for the construction of gender or Virginia Woolf's discussion of the relationship between women and fiction. More important, however, is the ability of my students to apply these theories to their lives. Whether in women's studies or art education, I want my students to be creators of feminist knowledge, not just receivers.

Critical theory itself is liberatory. Critical pedagogy aspires to be liberatory; however, at this point it too is mostly theoretical. Therefore it may be delivered, ironically, via authoritarian means because critical pedagogy has only partly fulfilled its charge: the teaching of methods for scrutinizing cultural production.

Feminist pedagogy, on the other hand, suffers from the opposite problem. Feminist teachers have developed methods for questioning cultural production but in the process have distanced themselves from content. Feminist pedagogical methods can serve all classes, all teachers, all students, and all forms of knowledge. Feminist pedagogy, however, is not a blanket methodology with which we can right all the ills of teaching. It is meaningful only if it links feminist theory and content. This distinguishes feminist pedagogy from other forms of "good teaching" (see Gaudelius, 1998, for an example of feminist theory and content in art-teaching practice).

Each of us, as we contemplate our pedagogical practices, needs to be self-reflective. Hoodfar advocates that teachers and students "locate themselves within the structure of the society" (p. 212). When critical and feminist theories inform our practice, and critical and feminist practice informs our theories, we have a model for liberatory education.

NOTES

[1]In the United States the development of feminist pedagogy is linked to the opening of women's studies programs throughout the country in the 1970s. Critical pedagogy is more closely linked to the antiwar and civil rights movements of the 1960s. Of course these movements interconnected but, although many women were involved in the civil rights and antiwar movements, few men were involved in the women's movement.

[2]In using Giroux as an example, I do not suggest that he is a canonical exemplar of critical pedagogy. Rather, I have chosen him because his work is widely read.

REFERENCES

Brady, J. (1995). *Schooling young children: A feminist pedagogy for liberatory learning*. Albany: State University of New York Press.

Freire, P. (1990). *Pedagogy of the oppressed*. M. B. Ramos, trans. New York: Continuum.

Gaudelius, Y. (1998). *Etudes féminine*: Hélène Cixous and an exploration of feminist pedagogy. In E. J. Sacca & E. Zimmerman, eds., *Women art educators IV: Herstories, ourstories, future stories* (pp. 170–181). Boucherville, Quebec: Canadian Society for Education Through Art.

Giroux, H. (1991). Modernism, postmodernism, and feminism: Rethinking the boundaries of educational discourse. In H. Giroux, ed., *Postmodernism, feminism, and cultural politics: Redrawing educational boundaries* (pp. 1–59). Albany: State University of New York Press.

Gore, J. M. (1993). *The struggle for pedagogies: Critical and feminist discourses as regimes of truth.* New York: Routledge.

Hoodfar, H. (1997). Feminist anthropology and critical pedagogy: The anthropology of classrooms' excluded voices. In S. de Castell & M. Bryson, eds., *Radical in<ter>ventions: Identity, politics, and difference/s in educational praxis* (pp. 211–232). Albany: State University of New York Press.

Kristeva, J. (1977). Stabat mater. L. S. Roudiez, trans. In T. Moi, ed., *The Kristeva reader* (pp. 161–186). New York: Columbia University Press.

Lewis, M. (1992). Interrupting patriarchy: Politics, resistance and transformation in the feminist classroom. In C. Luke & J. Gore, eds., *Feminisms and critical pedagogy* (pp. 167–191). New York: Routledge.

Lusted, D. (1986). Why pedagogy? An introduction to this issue. *Screen, 27* (5), 2–14.

Walkerdine, V. (1992). Progressive pedagogy and political struggle. In C. Luke & J. Gore, eds., *Feminisms and critical pedagogy* (pp. 15–24). New York: Routledge.

Weiler, K. (1988). *Women teaching for change.* New York: Bergin & Garvey.

CHAPTER 4

Deconstructing Media Images of Postmodern Childhood

PAUL DUNCUM

Art educators have moved past the view that childhood is a time of unbridled creativity, but many still consider children, simply, as constructivist learners (Efland, 1990). Many perceive childhood as a time singularly devoted to acquiring knowledge about the world. In a typically modernist shift, one metaphorical construct has merely replaced another. Both constructs presuppose that children possess easily identified, essentialist, universal natures. Many art educators continue to regard the nature of childhood as unproblematic.

Postmodern theorists, on the other hand, suggest that childhood consists of complex, fragmented, multiple identities (James & Prout, 1990). Rather than possessing a universal nature, postmodernists see childhood as an intersection of social perceptions, some with long precedents (Cunningham, 1995) but with no essential core. These conceptions extend our definitions of childhood from threatening presence to innocent victim, from rabid consumer to violent criminal (Duncum, 1997; Jenks, 1996).

The implications for art education are far-reaching. Here I describe two: children as grist for aesthetic manipulation and children's knowledge of violence and sex. My approach is through visual mass media presentations of these conceptions. Both conceptions, however incompatible, represent deeply held views of childhood. Each challenges us, as adults and as art educators, to examine our views.

THE IMPORTANCE OF CHILDHOOD

Some psychologists use the notion of the child within as an axiomatic metaphor of our psychic structures (Holland, 1992). The child we once were coexists with our adult identities, and we carry into adulthood childhood's unfinished business. Psychologists influenced by Freud suggest that the world of the unconscious is the world of metaphorical childhood—a world of pleasure, chaos, violence, and vulnerability (Harris, 1972). Adulthood, by contrast, means rationality, morality, and control. Because this requires repressing the "inferiority" of the child, we struggle to resist irrationality and emotionalism. Because childhood behaviors can persist into adulthood, we at times respond to provocation with the frustration and misplaced anger of children. Thus the child within threatens our adult status, and we devise measures to defend against this. Efforts to divide childhood from adulthood stem from adults' desires to protect themselves by controlling childhood (Holland, 1992). These desires to control childhood are not only about controlling actual children but also about controlling the child within.

The pressures of adulthood, including working with children, devalue children's positive qualities. Consequently adults may create idealized childhoods for themselves. If they cannot do that, they may create ideals of childhood. Childhood becomes a mythical place, a rich depository for qualities we have lost and long to recover. This results in what J. Kitzinger (1990) calls a "fetishistic glorification" of childhood (p. 160). Nowhere is this more apparent than in our present preoccupation with the notion of the aesthetic child.

THE AESTHETIC CHILD

Aesthetic children are hot sales items, as a visit to a gift shop will confirm. Images of children as objects of sensory delight are commonplace on cards, calendars, datebooks, posters, writing, and wrapping paper. Anne Geddes is perhaps the best-known artist in this genre. One of her photographs shows a small child with bright eyes and chubby cheeks squatting among lily pads framed by exotic flowers. In another a happy, naked baby rolls about on a bed of pink roses. Newborns sleep in pea pods. One naked newborn sleeps peacefully atop a pumpkin, another on a giant toadstool. Yet another lies curled amid a string of pearls on an oyster shell.

Few kinds of images challenge our professionalism more, because they employ aesthetic stratagems for arguably pathological purposes. Aestheticism concentrates on an artifact's potential to convey sensory pleasure while it ignores the conditions of the artifact's production (Williams, 1983). Aestheticism occurs when adults render children aesthetic. Aesthetic children embody beauty and fantasy. Mass media offer us these images for our sensory pleasure. They often stimulate nostalgic yearnings for happier, more secure times or indulgence in sweet, escapist fantasies. All portray children's bodies as items of pleasure, and commonly we take pleasure in their costumes and settings as well.

Aestheticizing childhood creates fantasies of children that have little to do with actual children. It changes the reality of children to fit a predetermined sensory pleasure. It demands the dominance of the image maker over the subject and invites viewers to participate in the dominance. To aestheticize children is to proffer a Peter Pan world where children never grow up. In a consumer society, where everything has a market value, consuming such images may seem a reasonable way to elicit lost love. The aestheticizing of childhood, then, can offer escape from the reality of actual children. Adults consume aesthetic images of children, seeking what real children may not give them—unquestioning, unwavering love.

John Bradshaw (1990) claims that many adults carry within them inner wounded children who can manifest themselves in adult pathologies such as objectifying and idealizing others. Images of aesthetic children objectify and idealize and thus can fill needs created by the wounded inner children within adults.

Aesthetic children are one of the most extreme forms of our persistent cultural belief in childhood innocence. The aesthetic child contrasts with the all-knowing child. The all-knowing child is as different from the aesthetic child as it is from the benign constructivist child.

THE ALL-KNOWING CHILD

Rarely is our traditional role as educators more undermined than with the concept of the all-knowing child. Traditional pedagogy rests on the assumption that children must learn knowledge selected by adults, but all-knowing children challenge this by teaching themselves whatever they desire to learn.

Images of children in front of computer screens have become commonplace. They of course appear in advertisements for computers but also in promotional materials of educational agencies from schools and other government entities. These images signify children's ready access to knowledge and means for economic progress.

Simultaneously, however, they signify access to violent and sexually explicit material at the push of a button—often a panic button for adults. Instant access to previously taboo knowledge challenges adults' beliefs about childhood innocence. Children sitting at computer screens can appear to be beyond adult supervision and thus beyond control—and thereby threatening.

Adults maintain the distinction between childhood and adulthood in part by adult ownership of cultural knowledge, perhaps especially about violence and sex (Jenks, 1996). Today this distinction is breaking down. In *The Disappearance of Childhood* Neil Postman (1983) argues that children of the 1980s were like children from the Middle Ages, when old and young shared all knowledge. With the invention of the printing press, he argues, knowledge became specialized and subject to censorship. Electronic media, however, have made nearly all knowledge accessible to all age groups (although not to all economic groups). These new media represent a return to visual and oral observation at the expense of text (Spender, 1994). Preprint societies are like our postprint society in making available to children knowledge that otherwise has been the particular purview of adults.

Whatever validity this broad-brush history might have, it is a commonplace among teachers and parents that children know more about the world than they did as children, including sexual knowledge. Moreover, children are often more adept than adults at accessing information technologically. The all-knowing child threatens a long-standing perception of childhood as innocent of violence and sex.

IMPLICATIONS FOR ART EDUCATION

The aesthetic child and the all-knowing child may challenge parents' and teachers' deeply held assumptions about childhood. They blur old boundaries. At best they signpost new, multifaceted views of childhood, and at worst, uncertainty about childhood, adulthood, and society itself. Since these issues involve images, they have far-reaching implications for art education.

Images of aesthetic and all-knowing children challenge our own adult views of children. Our schools support familiar beliefs that now demand reexamination. This can be sobering as well as enlightening because we deal with our most intimate selves, especially if we are parents or educators.

In school teachers perceive children as earnest, incomplete adults in need of correction. What has changed is what we must correct. The concept of the all-knowing child suggests that we dispense with top-down teaching and develop new pedagogy. Electronic media are to a degree replacing teachers as primary sources of knowledge. Kerry Freedman (1997) suggests that in schools students can try to make sense, face-to-face with others, of the media. She claims that media experiences are largely monological, in that making responses is the only form of engagement. The advantage of schools is that they allow experiences to generate meaning through dialogue. In other words, in school students can make dialogical sense of their monological environments. Art teachers' challenge is to guide children in learning they are already undertaking, and the focus is no longer on providing skills and knowledge but on developing values. Today's question is: whose values?

Images of children are resources for discussing with children how they see themselves positioned within society and the extent to which they accept, negotiate, or resist these positions. Do children, for example, find images of aesthetic children acceptable? Do they duplicate adult views with images of aesthetic children younger than they but resist when the children are their age? I have heard twelve-year-olds say in class that they would dislike seeing their siblings posed in Geddes's photographs. Edmund Feldman (1972) long ago advocated comparative studies of depictions of children as a major art historical theme. Comparing images of children past and present may highlight the special character of contemporary images and the social conditions that produce them.

These images exemplify a need for art educators to adopt a socially responsible role that extends beyond traditional curricular concerns. Knowledge of imagery is the core of any claim we could make to professional expertise. It is not ours exclusively, but it lies at the heart of the art educational enterprise. We are experts on images and responsible toward children; therefore, we must speak out about images that dehumanize children. Because images of aesthetic and all-knowing children prey on powerful psychological needs, we must point out their pathology.

Today's numerous and contradictory perceptions of children can confound and confront. They suggest that childhood comprises fragmented identities of which the constructivist learner is only one. Only by including these fragmented perceptions in our teaching can educators deal with children as whole people. Our first step is to acknowledge childhood's multiple realities to ourselves.

REFERENCES

Bradshaw, J. (1990). *Homecoming: Reclaiming and championing your inner child*. New York: Bantam.

Cunningham, H. (1995). *Children and childhood in Western society since 1500*. London: Longman.

Duncum, P. (1997). Cards, calendars, and the revival of the aesthetic child. *Collaborative Inquiry in a Postmodern Era: A Cat's Cradle, 2* (2), 53–68.

Efland, A. D. (1990). *A history of art education: Intellectual and social currents in teaching visual arts*. New York: Teachers College.

Feldman, E. B. (1972). *Varieties of visual experience*. New York: Abrams.

Freedman, K. (1997). Curriculum inside and outside school: Representation of fine art in popular culture. *Journal of Art and Design Education, 16* (2), 137–145.

Harris, T. (1972). *I'm OK: You're OK*. London: Pan.

Holland, P. (1992). *What is a child? Popular images of childhood*. London: Virago.

James, A., & Prout, A., eds. (1990). *Constructing and reconstructing childhood: Contemporary issues in the sociological study of childhood*. London: Falmer.

Jenks, C. (1996). *Childhood*. London: Routledge.

Kitzinger, J. (1990). Who are you kidding? Children, power, and the struggle against sexual abuse. In A. James & A. Prout, eds., *Constructing and reconstructing childhood: Contemporary issues in the sociological study of childhood* (pp. 157–183). London: Falmer.

Postman, N. (1983). *The disappearance of childhood*. New York: Delacorte Press.

Spender, D. (1994). A history of information media. *Australian Journal of Computing, 9* (1), 11–16.

Williams, R. (1983). *Keywords: A vocabulary of culture and society* (2nd ed.). London: Fontana.

Real-World Aesthetics: Breaking the Rules

KRIS FEHR

The authors in Part II break the rules. They've taught long enough that they can look up from their lecture notes about the Western canon and see the Hispanic faces, the black faces, the Asian faces, and the female faces staring blankly back at them. Where is their art? Where are they in the art world? Who makes these decisions? And who really cares, anyway?

"Can I get some water?"

"I need to go to the bathroom."

"Do we have to make a value scale again?"

When we teach, we set the boundaries of what our students call art. What we teach reveals our aesthetic theories, our ideas of what is valuable. Excluding the art of entire groups from what is valuable can result in serious consequences for students, who may react with lack of interest, aggression, or self-hatred. In this section teachers tell us ways to include our students' everyday experiences in their art and draw them into lively participation. Part II helps us examine our aesthetic theories. It helps us break the rules.

The first chapter in Part II, "Gender Politics in the Back Seat of a Lowrider," describes a common scenario: a new, idealistic teacher finds herself unprepared for the realities of her inner-city school. Her classroom is chaotic, and her students don't want to hear what she has to say. She turns to one of her professors, Dennis Earl Fehr, for help. Together they devise an art curriculum based on lowrider cars that honors her students' artistic heritage while drawing their attention to the sexism in lowrider culture. Fehr's deliberate use of a conversational format, informal English, and humor reflect his commitment to making scholarship engaging and relevant to our classroom practice.

Why are so many art teachers caught between the aesthetics their professors taught them and the ordinary interests of their students? In "Unmasking Ordinary Experience in Art," Grace Deniston-Trochta explores the transmission of "superior" aesthetic taste from faculty to students, exposing the myth of high art. Using her students' reactions to Precious Moments figurines, she examines the biases art students develop in their art studies, and the masks they use to hide their own tastes in favor of their professors'. She suggests that the best teachers show students "how broad and varied aesthetic space can be" by teaching diverse aesthetic values, including those of everyday experience.

When teachers insist on teaching only mainstream art, students suffer. In "Mountain Culture: No Hillbillies Here," Christine Ballengee Morris powerfully illustrates this problem by describing the experiences of relocated Appalachian Mountain children who study art that ignores or denigrates their culture. If these children give in to school pressure to internalize mainstream aesthetics, they lose their ties to their traditions, and in some cases they develop self-hatred. This chapter will interest not only teachers whose classrooms contain Appalachian students but also teachers who want a safe way to explore stereotypes, power, and identity.

In "You Don't Need a Penis to Be a Genius," Deborah Smith-Shank uses the in-your-face language of the Guerrilla Girls to draw our attention to the art world's gender inequality. She makes clear that genius is not gender linked, however much some people believe it is, and she describes women's genius and heroism in their struggles to become artists. She suggests that art curricula incorporate feminist art issues such as aging, reproductive rights, motherhood, and standards of beauty.

CHAPTER 5

Gender Politics in the Back Seat of a Lowrider

DENNIS EARL FEHR

The four reconstructed conversations in this chapter are based on actual conversations I had with an art teacher frustrated by her first job in an inner-city school. I use a conversational format, informal English, and humor for political reasons: I feel that this approach narrows the gap between scholarship and classroom experience—the theme of this book.

CONVERSATION ONE

"I'm afraid becoming an art teacher was a mistake!"

Alicia and I sat on the white stone bank of the Llano River where it winds through the green and red hills of Texas Tech University's Center at Junction.[1] A recent graduate of an out-of-state art education program, Alicia had returned to Houston, her childhood home, and was now teaching in a Chicano inner-city middle school in an East Side barrio. She was beginning her master's course work in art education this summer. Today was the first day of class. I had suggested that the students approach me if they wanted to discuss their teaching situations, and she had immediately sought me out.

D: Describe your typical teaching day, Alicia. Vent your frustrations. Then we'll look for reasons and form solutions.

A: It's chaos! They just run wild. Half of them don't speak English. Or they pretend not to. Although they seem to have the F word figured out. One of them called me a bitch on the last day of school. To my face! They couldn't care less about learning art. They leave the room anytime they want. I can tell they're saying bad things about me in Spanish. They think it's funny. It's so different from when I went to school!

D: What kinds of schools did you attend?

A: St. John's through eighth grade, then Bellaire High School. Bachelor of Fine Arts degree from Dartmouth. I've had a protected life. My parents bought me a three-story house for a college graduation present.

D: St. John's, Bellaire, Dartmouth, and a free house—not what I'd call deprived. The school you're in now has given you a dose of the real world, and you've fallen into a trap—you've adopted the traditional approach you saw around you, an approach bound up in authority, classroom control, teacher as expert, students as empty heads. Your students don't seem impressed with your curriculum. Did they have a voice in creating it?

A: Why would they? They don't know art the way I do.

D: Maybe they don't care about your curriculum because they don't see how it connects to their lives. For all intents your curriculum doesn't exist in your classroom. The real curriculum—the events that occur daily—is determined by them. The problem is not that they have no voice; it's that they have to use a subversive voice. And because they're challenging the domination of European art forms, they enact a curriculum of chaos.

A: How can I subvert their subversion? I feel like resigning.

D: I doubt that you'll resign. We can fix this. What are your students' interests?

A: We can fix this? I'll tell you what they're interested in—gangs, machismo, sex, and lowriders. They even have lowrider bicycles. Actually, some of the bikes are beautiful. I'd almost call them art. Not serious art, of course.

D: Not serious art? Hold that thought. First, are you describing the boys' and girls' interests equally?

A: I guess the boys', mostly.

D: Why?

A: I don't know. I didn't realize it. The boys' interests are more . . . noticeable.

D: How about teaching art about that? Are the boys louder?

A: Much.

D: What if you could teach art lessons that would hold your students' attention and at the same time cause them to question their gender assumptions?

A: How would I teach art about that?

D: If we listen to our students, they will listen to us. Art is both our vehicle and our priority, as lowrider bikes are to your students. You said lowrider bikes are almost art. Let's see if perhaps they are art, period, and if we can teach with them. I noticed some lowrider magazines on the rack at the grocery store in town. And some magazines for young Chicana women too. Would you be willing to buy a couple?

A: Where's the grocery store?

D: At Junction's only stoplight. Do you want to do that today and meet with me tomorrow?

A: Yes. Shall we meet here after class again?

D: Yes. We can't ask your students for their input from here, but we picked this topic on the basis of your observations of them. They're likely to go for it.

A: May I ask a question? Why would I teach lowrider art, since they learn that on their own? What about serious art like the Sistine Chapel or impressionism or Picasso? I barely have time to teach that, let alone this . . . folk art or whatever it is.

D: The way things are, you don't appear to be teaching your students anything, so let's teach something that interests them. We'll call this lesson Gender Politics in the Back Seat of a Lowrider. I'm looking forward to developing the art content tomorrow.

CONVERSATION TWO

D: Look, Alicia. Deer! Five of them. No, six.

A: Oh—there they go. And yesterday I saw my first armadillo. Well, my first live one. I walked up to about five feet from it.

D: Have you ever seen a campus like this?

A: Never. What a way to study art. The studio for my glassblowing class next session is outdoors by the meadow where the deer graze in the morning and evening. It's great.

D: So what did you find at the magazine store?

A: Two magazines. This one's called *Vajito.* It's a lowrider magazine full of photos of women in bikinis poking their fannies at us in front of cool cars. Here's another one, *Que Linda,* which is aimed at Chicana girls. Interestingly, *Que Linda* has even more photos of women in bikinis.

D: What does that teach?

A: Looks like *Vajito* teaches young men that women are sex objects, and *Que Linda* teaches young women that women are sex objects. I see your point about discussing that in junior high, but I'm worried about parental and administrative disapproval.

D: Yes, that's something to consider. In my ten years as a junior high art teacher, I developed strategies for teaching provocative art. I made clear our academic purpose and kept local standards in mind. I taught in a conservative community and never had a problem. In the case of your lesson, complaining parents would find themselves arguing in favor of women being displayed in degrading ways. My experience guarantees nothing, though, so the decision is yours.

A: Your experience points the way for me. I'll go for it. Now another problem—I'm still not sure I would be teaching art.

D: Let's find out. What is an aspect of art that can be taught with lowriders?

A: Well, art elements and design principles. But you said in class that art ed needs to be more than that.

D: Yes. Remember that throughout this unit on lowrider art, you and your students are discussing the legitimacy of lowriders as art, and why girls and boys deserve equal respect. That's weighty content. Let's start with elements and principles and expand from there. Notice the abstract designs in the paint job on this pickup truck. That looks like an intro to the theme of abstraction in art. How far back does abstraction go?

A: To prehistoric designs.

D: Good. Prehistoric images may be the earliest roots of lowrider designs. What other art emphasizes abstract designs?

A: Native American pottery. Greek vases. African masks. Op art. Geometry in quilt patterns. Geometry in math class.

D: Great answer—lots of possibilities. What are some popular Chicano art forms besides lowriders?

A: The images of *Dia de los Muertos* and *Cinco de Mayo*. The art of the Catholic church. The Virgin of Guadalupe.

D: Right, and you also could teach about the Chicano art movement of the 1960s and its evolution to today. These artists could be their role models.

A: I don't know if those would be appropriate role models.

D: Don't worry. People don't select role models who do things they don't value. If students learn to value equality, they will select artists who represent that. I'm more concerned about moving the focus away from the populist art forms your students have in their homes. Or garages, in the case of lowriders.

A: I know of Diego Rivera and Frida Kahlo. I can't think of other Mexican artists. Since we are sitting on what used to be Mexico, I should know more.

D: Off the top of my head I can think of Ana Mendieta, Frank Romero, Yolanda Lopez, Roberto Salas, Tina Modotti, John Hernandez, Maria Izquierdo, and John Valadez. Of course *Los Tres Grandes*—Diego Rivera, Jose Orozco, and David Siquieros. Texas artists such as Carmen Lomas Garza, Jesus Morales, and Luis Jiminez. And others just as good; I can't name all of them. So how should we start?

A: With lowriders. I could laminate photos from *Vajito*.

D: Are they big enough?

A: No, but what else can I do?

D: You could scan them into a computerized slide program. How about if you and your students create a slide presentation in PowerPoint or some program like that? That way they would construct the knowledge rather than sit passively while you present it to them. Does your school have the technology?

A: We could do it in the computer lab, but art classes don't have regularly scheduled use of the lab.

D: Could you request lab time for this unit?

A: I could schedule a meeting with my principal and the technology teacher to explain my plan. Maybe they would let my class research artists and present what they learned using the technology in our lab.

D: They would probably like that idea. Remind them that the world is communicating more and more with visual imagery rather than written text. Point out that successful people in the twenty-first century will be literate in visual as well as verbal language. You could start out your lowrider unit by discussing which images to scan. Ask them to write why they selected their images, and record their reasons on a large chart. Use their language—exactly how they wrote. That can become part of your text in the PowerPoint presentation.

A: I'll bet my vice principal would help me out. She's been wonderful—a true art lover. I wish the teachers felt that way. At our last faculty meeting a reading teacher wondered if some art time could be given up for reading skill drills to prepare students for the Texas Assessment of Academic Skills test. She complained that students today are becoming less and less literate.

D: Think about that. What kind of literacy was she talking about, visual or verbal?

A: Verbal.

D: Right. Humans relied on pictographs until written language was invented about six thousand years ago. It partially replaced visual language because in some ways it better suited the needs of early civilization.

Only in the last century and a half has visual language begun to reclaim its place, with cameras, movies, TV, and now computers. Many educators and politicians don't understand that this trend may make art a major school subject in the next century.

Recently on *Firing Line* I watched three conservatives, William Buckley, James Kilpatrick, and John Simon, bemoaning "the decline of Western civilization" because we now are learning more from images and less from text. They don't understand that the movement toward visual literacy is not creating imbalance—it is correcting it. Overall, kids are as literate as ever. Buckley, the host, should have had a couple of art teachers on his show instead of Kilpatrick and Simon. Then the audience might have learned something.

A: I agree. Rapidly changing images seem to mark our era, and I see why I should include technology in this unit. But I still don't understand how I can include ethical problems such as sexism.

D: By linking art to social and ethical issues, we breathe life into it. That doesn't mean we dilute our art teaching. Art questions society. Art addresses why drugs gnaw society's bones, why the gap between rich and poor grows wider, why the religious right imposes its vision on our schools, why reports of child abuse increase, why the "me first" side of capitalism is ignored, and why hate in the forms of racism, sexism, and homophobia does more damage than drugs.

Fine, you say, but how can we address sexism in this lowrider unit? By forgetting the European fine art canon for now. It does not encompass the world's greatest art; it encompasses only the greatest art made by European men. That may amount to 1 percent of the world's greatest art.

Then teach media literacy strategies from the mass communications field. Some graduates of mass communications work for politicians or the corporate world as experts in swaying public opinion. Part of our responsibility is to teach resistance to their visual messages. We need to teach our students that Madison Avenue definitions of hipness are fictions that empty their wallets by preying on their insecurities.

A: Okay, Dennis, what do I do with this ad in *Que Linda* for a female singing group? In this photo they're wearing black lingerie, and in this one, small towels draped over their breasts. What do these images have to do with music?

D: Not much. They're about women as sex toys. Notice that both magazine covers feature seductively dressed women. The subscription ad for *Vajito* features a woman in skimpy attire and the woman in the

Que Linda ad is nude. Here's a T-shirt ad in *Que Linda*. The model's T-shirt is wet. What's the message?

A: Women should seduce with their bodies. And look at this insert—pages of women with breast implants modeling skimpy bikinis and underwear. In a magazine for young women. I'm going to show these ads to my streetwise junior high students. I'll get snorting from the guys at first, but I'll bet it goes away when I start asking questions and they realize how narrowly these images define not only their female classmates but them too for seeing women one-dimensionally. Then we could find images that empower women. We could teach gender politics by replacing images of women in bikinis standing next to cars with women in boardrooms standing next to profit charts.

D: That promotes another patriarchal value, but it's a start. Our radical goal is a world in which we value nurturing, sharing, and collaboration. You probably will observe some positive change resulting from this lesson, but the grunting won't go away quickly. It will take more than one lesson for many of your boys and girls to comprehend the dehumanizing effect of images that some of them have been viewing favorably for years. This lesson must be regarded as the first step of many. Ethical issues such as gender politics must become a linchpin of art education in general.

A: I see how this unit can get them to process these issues. Now what kind of studio project would be appropriate?

D: This fall ask your students what they want to do. They may come up with a great idea.

CONVERSATION THREE

D: Alicia, good to hear from you. Hard to believe two months have passed since our class in Junction. How did it feel to return to Houston?

A: I didn't realize how much I had missed the gridlock, crime, and urban blight until I got back to it.

D: I understand. Are you trying out the lowrider curriculum?

A: Yes! The students love it, and I'm thrilled. I've had only one behavior disruption the entire week we've been doing it, and I didn't even have a chance to deal with it—the class jumped on this poor kid's case, and he's been an angel ever since. Hey, can you think of anyone who wants to give away a car?

D: Gosh, usually I can think of dozens, but today not a soul. Why?

A: I asked the students what they wanted to do for a studio component of the unit. They want to enter a car in Houston's Art Car Parade.

D: Great idea! Does it have to be a lowrider?

A: That would be great, but beggars can't be choosers. Oh, and I asked my vice principal about computer lab time for art. We start next week.

D: Your students are fortunate that you're their teacher. This unit will teach them that lowrider art with its intricate geometric abstractions deserves respect from everyone, while the presentation of this art form with nearly naked women equates the women with the cars—just objects of desire. It's nice to be desired by someone you desire in return, but an object has no control over who does the desiring. That may be one of the most valuable lessons a person can learn in twelve years of school. And my best wishes on getting the car. Knowing you, you'll get one.

CONVERSATION FOUR

D: Hi, Alicia. Nice to hear from you.

A: Likewise. Hey, guess what? You're going to love this.

D: What?

A: We got a car!

D: A real car? Steering wheel? Seats? Doors?

A: Even an AM radio. Doesn't work, but it's there.

D: So who gave you a car?

A: My vice principal came through again. She had an old junker with high mileage that she was going to trade in, but they offered her only $200. She said she would just give it to us and write it off her taxes.

D: Fantastic. Now what are you going to do with the car for the parade?

A: The president of the Art Club is a girl. She's going to wear a business suit and sit in the back seat. The vice president is a boy. He's going to wear a servant's outfit. He'll hold the door for her and drive her in the parade. Get it? We're deconstructing traditional gender roles.

D: I love it! Of course you're maintaining socioeconomic disparities, but that can be Lesson Two.

A: So far all we've done to the car is hang a pair of red dice from the rearview mirror and put a toy puppy in the back window. Its head bounces when you drive. The students voted to paint the car gold—tires, bumpers, everything but the glass. Do you think we'll win first prize?

D: I'm an artist—let me visualize it. Louise Nevelson painted some of her wooden assemblages gold, and they're displayed in major museums. Why not a gold car? Yes, you'll win! I'll bet a paycheck on it.

A: Whose?

D: Yours.

NOTES

[1]Texas Tech University's rural campus at Junction, Texas, offers master's degrees in art education in an intense summers-only program granting one credit hour per week.

CHAPTER 6

Unmasking Ordinary Experience in Art

GRACE DENISTON-TROCHTA

In an art education course for future teachers I suggested that the popular series of figurines known as Precious Moments reflects many people's aesthetic values. Their commercial success is perhaps due to their sentimental iconography. Most of my students ridiculed the "preciousness" of these figurines. However, one student confessed that she liked them, and that she owned a collection of them.

All hell broke loose. Her classmates' merciless taunts revealed assumptions that their taste was superior to that of others. By pointing this out, I guided my students to see how their prejudices closed avenues for discourse with those whose definitions differed from theirs. By recognizing that they were bullying a classmate to accept their borrowed bias, they began to understand art as social practice.

Critiquing art as social practice can expose how it perpetuates cultural prejudices. It can reveal why we acquiesce to the power of the norm by disguising ourselves with masks and performance. In their newfound awareness, my students discovered their ambivalence about Precious Moments. They removed the masks they had learned to wear when their art professors disparaged the students' aesthetic tastes.

This frank discussion occurred because we expanded our definitions of aesthetic acceptability to include our personal experiences, and we recognized the social class asymmetry embedded in the art world's aesthetic standards. In this chapter I describe how my students reconsidered aesthetics, not as a membership badge to an inner circle, but as part of being human.

THE MANNER OF MASKS AND MASQUERADES

A mask is a false display. I use the term *mask* to mean concealment of the self for protection. It is camouflage, like the fur of the snowshoe hare that turns white in winter—it is about survival, even if only in terms of getting a prized grade. Sometimes it conceals shame over the perception that one's understanding of art is inadequate. An entire class can be in masquerade, the faces pretending agreement, because masks have the power to influence others to don them.

The Mask as Mirror

My students' masks took several forms, one of which mirrors the "superior" tastes of their professors. One student confessed to wearing this type of mask when he "enthusiastically" mirrored his professors' views. He felt that he had become a favorite among the faculty, he self-consciously admitted. Other students spoke of how they simply mastered the art of imitation to pass their studio classes.

The Mask of Silence

Another mask my students wore was that of silence. Some described how they employed silence to resist imposed standards of beauty. One student used silence by not revealing until after our discussion that he had purchased a Precious Moments bride and groom set for his wedding cake.

Others used silence to cover their embarrassment at being unable to value aesthetic objects their professors presented. These objects required a code they felt unable to crack. Silence hid fear as well—fear of being wrong in classes where honest inquiry was less important than passing along a predetermined aesthetic legacy.

The Deadly Mask of Cultural Assimilation

My Hispanic students have brought to my attention another kind of mask. They call this mask the mask of the Anglo. Like the other masks, this mask is worn selectively—in particular, in situations in which they feel pressured to embrace an aesthetic hierarchy unlike their own. The shape of this mask is of superficial deference to an Anglo legacy.

Hispanic students tend to be raised Roman Catholic and are exposed to the church's rich iconographic heritage. This iconography contains highly expressive visual symbols. Steeped in this imagery from my own childhood, I remember images of the sacred heart of Jesus, dripping blood, pierced with thorns—not for the weak of heart, if you'll forgive the expression. Nor are the stigmata of St. Francis of Assisi or images of the Blessed Virgin stepping on a snake in the defeat of evil.

Frida Kahlo used such images in her paintings. The pleasure of my Hispanic students in studying her revealed the importance of religious imagery in their lives. This iconography has everything to do with aesthetics. It is sentimental at times, as life itself can be. In Anglo society, Hispanic students can be coerced into leaving behind this aesthetic heritage, which means loss of power, insight, joy, and social perspective.

Unlike Catholic religious iconography, Precious Moments figurines are intended as a strictly commercial enterprise. However, they too acquire meaning. For some they mean brightness in a dark world. They provide community for collectors. For some they represent admirable values that society is losing. And for some they provide leisure diversion. Their sentimentality is for some their most valued quality.

For harsh judges of sentimentality, Precious Moments figurines are markers of class asymmetry. These judges may deny the meaning these figures hold for some. They may refuse to acknowledge the ethically troubling social hierarchies created by their notions of aesthetic superiority. I want my students to identify these mechanisms of status and class exploitation. I also want my students to identify their own aesthetic symbols.

Religion, social class, ethnicity, and aesthetics are linked. Acknowledging broad aesthetic definitions is part of respecting cultural diversity. Symbols that are unappealing to some may touch the hearts of others with hope, joy, and love. For that they are to be respected by all, which brings me full circle to my class's discussion on masks.

I recognize my students' masks because I wore them as a student (through an entire doctoral program, in fact) and again as a teacher. I wore these masks during my adolescence as a first-generation American whose aesthetics did not resonate with the aesthetics of my schooling. Other kinds of masks exist, but I have recognized the masks I mentioned here particularly in female students and colleagues.[1]

THE EFFECTS OF MASKING

When we demean our students' aesthetic symbols, we insure that they will wear masks. Will they glitter back a teacher's self-importance through artful mimicry? Will they silently frustrate us as we attempt class discussions? Will we coconspire as together we deny their heritages by adopting white, middle-class tastes?

My students recognized that the time and energy needed to wear masks took away from discovering the social origins of their tastes and the meanings within those origins. In the shadows of our culture's dominant aesthetic and the pageant of expertise that upholds it, student experience becomes insignificant, social distinctions are unrecognized, and aesthetic breadth is devalued. Topologies are not questioned, and didactic teachers maintain their enthroned positions as undisputed masters of taste.

Ordinary Life and Ordinary Experience

Within academic art discourse the sentimental is derogatory. However, the sentimental is born in "ordinary" experience and therefore is an aesthetic of the ordinary. As an aesthetic, it may help us celebrate experience, make meaning, and recognize social realities.

As our students hide from those who claim aesthetic ownership, ordinary experience is devalued. Some of my students admitted that they were drawn to art and adopted "superior" taste in order to distinguish themselves from their peers. One student claimed that choosing an art profession secured his identity as "someone special." Unfortunately, this gain of "cultural capital" bypasses the aesthetic. Teachers may make little effort to connect art to students' experiences or aesthetic values, to say nothing of the social origins of these values. Such hoarding of cultural capital simply creates more masks and leads the mask wearers away from the full meanings, pleasures, and transcendence that the visual arts provide.

The Sentimental as Derogatory

Derogating the sentimental diminishes ordinary life. Common, daily pursuits may not be as ordinary as they appear. Furthermore, the specific aesthetic sensibilities of social class are not as flexible as we might believe.[2]

Considering the presence of sentimentality in the art of all cultures, the art world applies the label *kitsch* to the work of many hands. This devalues ordinary life in spite of the fact that it is sometimes more richly textured than abstractions of aesthetic values.

Aesthetic Knowing

"It is as dangerous to attribute . . . a systematic aesthetic to . . . ordinary people as it is to adopt . . . the strictly negative conception of ordinary vision which is the basis of every 'high' aesthetic" (Bourdieu, 1984, p. 32). Art students learn the aesthetics of the "best" art throughout the history of "mankind." This assumes that aesthetics designed by the ruling class must be learned. Yet my students don masks when demanded to adapt aesthetics unlike their own. This may not be the most beneficial kind of knowing to gain from aesthetic study.

Aesthetic knowing can be described as a lifelong conversation. Many artists document this in journals and letters. Examples include the memoirs of Faith Ringgold (1995), the letters of Vincent van Gogh (1929), and the diaries of Käthe Kollwitz (Winston, 1955). Those who have taught children of diverse cultural backgrounds recognize that aesthetic knowing begins before kindergarten. Those who have taught older populations recognize that aesthetic knowing is a lifelong process that gives meaning to experience (including the realities of aging).

To paraphrase Parker Palmer (1998), "[Aesthetic knowing] is an eternal conversation about things that matter, conducted with passion and discipline" (p. 104). A conversation is not a systematic body of knowledge to be learned.

Problematizing "Knowledge" as Pedagogy

Because we place aesthetic sentimentality at the bottom of our cultural hierarchy of values, we seldom examine it. Its incompatibility with systematic aesthetics allows the art world to ignore it. Systematic aesthetics are valued for their presumed neutrality, universality, formulae, and purity, but Paulo Freire (1990) urged teachers and students to consider knowledge problematic and to ask whose interests it serves. Critical pedagogy pulls back veils that obscure agendas behind academic "realities." We fail to realize that honoring sentimentality does not imply accepting it as our own aesthetic. It does mean acknowledging its value to others.

CONCLUSION

What alternatives do we have to learning systematic aesthetics from teachers who have already decided what is good? We can learn from teachers who respect our aesthetics, who show us how broad and varied aesthetic space can be. I learned from such a teacher — Marilyn Zurmuehlen. She increased her students' aesthetic space by creating aesthetic meaning from our experiences. Using anecdotes about her niece and nephews, she modeled a curriculum of the ordinary. By taking our experiences seriously, Marilyn gave us room to go beyond the aesthetic frames of academia to develop our own aesthetic criteria.

By acknowledging complexity and refusing orthodoxy, we create hope for art education. We can convey our awareness of complexity (for example, the asymmetry of social relations) to our students. We can convey how aesthetic knowing is a lifelong conversation and how our daily lives continuously call forth aesthetic responses. By framing the aesthetic as conversation, we can respect our students' choices rather than impose our own. Our respect encourages them to explore messy terrain. Framed in this way, aesthetic knowing can become "an eternal conversation about things that matter, conducted with passion and discipline." Its referent is humankind, not systematized aesthetic principles.

Meaning is determined in part by cultural codes. These codes may control us without intervention, trapping us on public stages as we "perform for our lives." Are we teaching our students to perform on the same stages? If so, we may be diminishing their "ordinary" aesthetic values. We who are fortunate enough to teach art can create aesthetic spaces broad enough for our students to build their own stages and write their own performances.

NOTES

[1]For an elaboration of this phenomenon, I recommend *Women's Ways of Knowing* by Belenky, Clinchy, Goldberger, and Tarule (1986).

[2]In her research on working-class families Valerie Walkerdine (1990) has elaborated on the presumptions of academics who judge working-class aesthetics.

REFERENCES

Belenky, M. F., Clinchy, B. M., Goldberger, N. R., & Tarule, J. M. (1986). *Women's ways of knowing: The development of self, voice, and mind.* New York: Basic Books.

Bourdieu, P. (1984). *Distinction: A social critique of the judgment of taste.* R. Nice, trans. Cambridge, MA: Harvard University Press.

Freire, P. (1990). *Pedagogy of the oppressed*. M. B. Ramos, trans. New York: Continuum.

Palmer, P. J. (1998). *The courage to teach: Exploring the inner landscape of a teacher's life*. San Francisco: Jossey-Bass.

Ringgold, F. (1995). *We flew over the bridge: The memoirs of Faith Ringgold*. Boston: Little, Brown.

van Gogh, V. (1929). *Further letters of Vincent van Gogh to his brother, 1886–1889*. London: Constable.

Walkerdine, V. (1990). *Schoolgirl fictions*. New York: Verso.

Winston, R. C., trans. (1955). *The diaries and letters of Käthe Kollwitz*. Chicago: Henry Regnery.

CHAPTER 7

Mountain Culture:
No Hillbillies Here

CHRISTINE BALLENGEE MORRIS

The hillbilly is a cartoon figure, alternately comedic or sinister, that contrasts with the people of Appalachian Mountain Culture to whom it refers. This image portrays Mountain people as lazy, stupid, sloppy, violent, moonshining, tobacco spitting, barefoot, and incestuous. In fact, Appalachian mountaineers possess no more of these attributes than any other group. Virtually every ethnic group in the United States can be on both the giving and receiving ends of demeaning stereotyping. The label *hillbilly* is as offensive as derogatory labels other groups endure. The difference is that many other labels are being revised with positive definitions. *Hillbilly* is not.

The stereotype has created image distortions in mainstream America, in academia, and among Mountain people themselves. This chapter is about Appalachian and non-Appalachian youth exploring the concept of hillbilly, developing cultural identities, and responding to stereotypes— all within the frame of art education. This research addresses the negotiation required of any group that encounters derogatory portrayals of itself. Consider this paper and its lesson plans as safe ways for Appalachian and non-Appalachian students to explore stereotypes, power, and identity.

Educators have important reasons to understand this culture and its arts. In the last quarter of the nineteenth century missionaries with preconceived ideas of the culture built schools in the region (Morris, 1997a). After World War II more than 650,000 Appalachians migrated[1] to other areas in the United States for work. This created an Appalachian minority (Morris 1997b). Since then, Mountain youth have had to cope with pedagogical styles that conflict with their traditional oral learning style.

Many Mountain children have been labeled behaviorally disordered for "being defiant." At the 1996 REACH (Realizing Ethnic Awareness and Cultural Heritage) conference an Appalachian writer for the *Dayton Daily* told his story[2] of struggling with the negative image. Fights and lack of interest in school were his responses.

Another speaker addressed her problems with the image as a child living in Detroit. School was an unpleasant place where she was labeled learning disabled. She ran home each day as soon as she could.

Recently in Newark, Ohio, a young man from Georgia was repeatedly shamed by his high school Spanish teacher for his Mountain accent. His grades dropped from As and Bs to barely passing. He responded by leaving his family in Ohio to live with his grandfather near Atlanta to raise his grades so he could attend college.

In Tazewell County, Virginia, an elementary student was labeled learning disabled and "in need of culture." This student is Cherokee Appalachian. She attends powwows, sings, dances, and creates art. She has been instructed in tribal spirituality. At tribal events she wears Cherokee clothing. She has had constant exposure to traditional Mountain arts as well. Yet she is "in need of culture." After two years of home schooling she was tested, and no learning disability was found. Story after story reveals psychic damage when the stereotype collides with cultural identity. In the eyes of these people, school was a painful experience that devalued them and their culture. They never forgot. Many cultural and ethnic groups have protested and educated society and the media about derogatory words and harmful stereotypic images. So far members of Appalachian Mountain Culture have been unsuccessful in bringing about this change.

STICKS AND STONES MAY BREAK...

Mountain Culture people are a hybridization of ethnic groups including Native Americans, Africans, and Scotch-Irish. They transmit culture by oral tradition (Morris, 1997b), a tradition improperly translated by some outsiders as meaning static (Hart, 1992–1993). In Mountain Culture, tradition is defined as a bridge between past and present informed by geography, occupations, social change, resistance to oppression, political dynamics, and stereotypical cultural representation (Morris, 1997b). Narrowly defining a culture leads to institutional stagnation. Mountain Culture is complex and hence defies generalization. Its art forms have followed regional changes and therefore vary widely. They include quilts, murals, sculptures made of recycled materials and animal bones, outdoor installations, baskets, glass-bead works, jug-head pottery, and musical instruments.

Stereotyping a culture is one way to control it. Stereotyping of Mountain Culture began after the Civil War when developers came into the region. They used education and the media to create ethnic and class stratification. The stereotyping continued with the social upheaval of the Industrial Revolution. Fear of change motivated outsiders to seek their pioneer roots. Writers, anthropologists, philanthropists, and collectors descended on Appalachia. A writing style called local color created stereotypes that still endure. The popular novels of John Fox Jr., for example, described Mountain people as savage, barbaric, and bloodthirsty (Smith, 1983).

The word *hillbilly* appeared in print in the *New York Journal* on April 23, 1900. The publication defined the term as "a free and untrammeled white citizen of Alabama, who lives in the hills, has no means to speak of, dresses as he can, talks as he pleases, drinks whiskey when he gets it, and fires off his revolver as the fancy takes him" (Green, 1965, p. 204). Some outsiders generalized such characterizations into a stereotype. bell hooks (1992) has explored stereotypes and believes they serve those in power. "Like fiction," hooks writes, "they are created to serve as a substitution, standing in for what is real. They are there not to tell it like it is but to invite and encourage pretense" (1992, p. 341).

Film and television carried the stereotype to a wide audience. In the 1950s and 1960s America saw its first televised images of Appalachian culture on the sitcom *The Real McCoys,* which debuted as the program *Amos and Andy* was canceled because of its stereotyped portrayal of African Americans. Other sitcoms followed: *Green Acres, Petticoat Junction, The Beverly Hillbillies,* and *The Andy Griffith Show.* These shows presented Mountain people as simple, backward moonshiners—outside mainstream culture's definition of normal. These portrayals led the public to see the stereotypes as true. Recently a student of mine said, "How can you say it is not true? Have you ever looked at them? They need to come off the mountains and quit inbreeding and catch up with the 1990s" (personal communication, May 10, 1988).

BUT WORDS CAN NEVER ... WHAT?

The need to critique popular perceptions of cultural identity is not just an Appalachian phenomenon. Any culture confronted with entrenched stereotypes of itself must grapple with self-hatred and cultural denial within its members. Many Native Americans, for example, have begun to explore Indianness—stereotyped representation, sports icons, and "Indian art." This exploration reached a critical mass in 1992, the five hundredth anniversary of Columbus's arrival in America. Native perspectives of this event were common in the media coverage.

In *Apples on the Flood* Cunningham (1987) concludes that internalizing a pejorative image can create infantilization. This seems to hinder some members of Mountain Culture—particularly the young—from accepting their identity. One Mountain Culture artist described his perspective as a youth:

> Back when I was growing up, it was during the Kennedy Era in West Virginia. It [the hillbilly image] directly affected a lot of people, at least it did me. I was ashamed of the way we were portrayed. We cooked with wood, and we heated with coal and had to take a bath in a damn washtub in the kitchen and stuff like that. It never really meant anything to me, and I was very satisfied with it until I saw the horror on the faces of the people in the United States when they were looking at pictures of the poor, backward Appalachians, and it suddenly occurred to me that the things that I'd been satisfied with all my life and felt good about as a youngster [were] probably something to be ashamed of, and I was. Very much so. I ran as hard as I could from West Virginia. Now I resent the people that caused me to do that. (Personal communication, September 20, 1993)

As a young adult he experienced conflict with his and outsiders' perceptions of his culture. The initial result was self-hatred. With time, community support, and a developing appreciation of Mountain art forms, he came to embrace his cultural identity. He believes youth need to hear stories like his to understand that they are not alone and that denying their culture is not the answer.

In this story, a Mountain family decides its culture is inferior:

> Because of outsiders' portrayal and value on Mountain Culture, my mother's generation had decided that the Mountain Culture was of no value, and they had thrown it out and tried to replace it with the Middle-Class American Culture. So I was digging through the trash, trying to dig up those people who had been discarded. It seems to me, when two cultures are side by side, you don't have the two coming

together and forming a third one—an alloy that is better and stronger. I
observe one seeking to destroy the other, or one of them clamps down
on the other in such a way that the other one can't get out from under
that. So the problem in the Mountain Culture I see is the people feeling
they're nothing, and that destroys you. Stereotypes are here, and we
have to live with, accept, or deny [them]. (Personal communication,
September 11, 1993)

Although this speaker has embraced his family's original cultural identity, he did so without their support. The foundation for his determination
was his desire to learn Mountain music, an art form that had touched
him. He believes other youth can find cultural identity through Mountain
arts and traditions. He started a program in a local high school to test this,
and his results were positive. He worked with behaviorally disruptive
boys. Each week he taught songs and music and told stories. The students' behavior and grades improved.

Cultural acceptance or denial can depend on individual situations. In
1995 John Nakishima produced and directed a documentary film, *Mountaineers*. Originally he intended to make a film about why many West
Virginians consider their state special, but he found that people wanted to
address the hillbilly image. One woman told of being asked if she were
Ellie Mae Clampett, a character from *The Beverly Hillbillies*. She responded angrily, "I was going to go off on her." Her choice to use the in-
digenous Mountain expression "go off" is similar to using the word
hillbilly defiantly—both are acts of self-determination.

Without positive alter images some Mountain Culture youth assimi-
late the hillbilly stereotype by default—"Oh my God, I'm a hillbilly!" In
interviewing students, I found that one of their main reasons for leaving
their region is to remake themselves into a more "positive, accepted
image because I don't want to grow up and be Ellie Mae." Even those
who embrace their cultural identity may have to deal with the hillbilly
image as they leave to seek employment.

A HILLBILLY IS . . . AND I'M A MOUNTAINEER!

Many Appalachian schools deal inadequately with Mountain children's
needs for recognition of their traditions. When I discuss Appalachian
Mountain Culture with students in fourth grade and above, they wish to
discuss the stereotype and experiences they have had with outsiders.
They reveal confusion, shame, and anger.

Public education in Mountain regions often supports the stereotype. Stated and unstated policies can lead to interpreting cultural differences as behavioral problems. In the *Columbus Dispatch,* May 17, 1998, Janet S. Fenholt, former executive director of the Ready to Read Literacy Program in Columbus, Ohio, responded to a headline implying that Ohio's increasing illiteracy was the fault of Appalachians. She concluded, "Illiteracy has many faces, and Appalachia is only one of them" (Price, 1998, p. 1A). The same edition carried a story about a lawsuit filed by a Mountain student from Perry County who was asking for equitable education funding. In the lawsuit the plaintiff suggested that illiteracy in Ohio's Appalachian region was due to the state's disregard for the area (Price, 1998, p. 1A).

Another factor is the omission of Mountain Culture in educational materials. In school curricula, Appalachians are invisible (Morris, 1997a). Some authors who include Mountain Culture (cf. Bice, 1995) refer to it as something to be observed rather than practiced. Studying cultures in schools can provide openings for exploring multiple perspectives, but outsiders traditionally have used education to control Mountain people. A 1912 editorial in the *New York Times* stated, "Mountaineers are like the Red Indians, they must learn. There are two remedies, education or extermination" (Smith, 1983). Such thinking remains.

Returning to cultural traditions such as stories, songs, ballads, dances, and visual arts can help students heal. Many Native American nations, for example, are returning to their traditions to resolve problems such as alcoholism, suicide, and drug abuse (Churchill, 1996). Similar problems exist in Appalachia. Not only can Mountain children benefit from studying their heritage, but all students can. These stories contain lessons on how to lead a life well lived. They offer the wisdom of history in addressing contemporary needs of both members and nonmembers of Mountain Culture.

A pedagogical goal is to connect old stories to present circumstances by comparing, questioning, and analyzing. From this students can learn to honor Mountain Culture, rebuild their world views, and bring about social change. This approach differs from linear, segregated educational models that present heritage as a time capsule packed with cultural relics (Giroux, 1993; Hart, 1992–1993; Morris, 1997a). Art education that presents culture as frozen diminishes oral traditions and nurtures cultural and self-hatred (Cunningham, 1987; Morris, 1997a). Eliot Wigginton (1972), editor of *The Foxfire Series,* found that when his Mountain students interviewed community elders, they acquired respect for their oral traditions, knowledge of their identity, self-reliance, and awareness of human interdependence. He also acknowledged that projects like his did not solve all problems. His students learned that confronting cultural stereotypes through art is not a one-time memorizing of facts and rules but a lifelong process of inquiry.

LESSON PLANS

I have guided Mountain students from primary grades to the university level in confronting the hillbilly image. I begin by showing examples of the image—postcards, Christmas cards, billboards, visual artwork, movies such as *Lil' Abner, Next of Kin,* and *The Beverly Hillbillies,* and television shows such as *The Beverly Hillbillies, The Waltons,* and *Christy.* My students write their impressions and discuss them. Anger and laughter are two immediate responses, but the conversation invariably turns to their personal stories.

At this point I show excerpts of documentaries about the hillbilly image such as *Mountaineers,* H. E. Smith's *Strangers and Kin* (1983), and J. Young's *Dancin' Outlaw.* In *Mountaineers* and *Strangers and Kin* artists discuss their explorations of the hillbilly image, cultural identity, Mountain arts, and positive resistance. The documentary *Dancin' Outlaw* illustrates how producers project cultural stereotypes as factual through editing and interview baiting.

Students need to go beyond content awareness to social action. My students design assignments to do this. Some have contacted the producers of these films to express their reactions. Some have written art curricula. All direct their passion toward changing social attitudes.

After students explore their topic historically, aesthetically, and critically, the next step is for them to react visually. They learn about their local art and artists from direct experience rather than from generic forms labeled Appalachian in books.[3] The *Museographs* series (Lazar Group, 1995), for example, shows baskets, instruments, whittled objects, and quilts, which are important art forms, but Appalachian art is broader than that. Here are some exploratory, social, action-based art projects that I have collected from art teachers:

1. Self-portraits that infuse photographs of the students with the hillbilly image.
2. Community portraits—group sculptural assemblages that illustrate a town and its people.

3. Cultural quilts that honor their makers by illustrating their values.
4. Portrait quilts that include photographic transfers and texts expressing the makers' definitions of self.
5. Life-sized portraits drawn and painted individually, then posed together to form a sculptured community.
6. Student-created plays and stage backdrops that honor Mountain Culture.
7. Videos that redefine Mountain Culture by showing interviews in which adults give advice to youth on dealing with the hillbilly image.
8. Handmade books that contain stories about adults' youthful trials with the hillbilly image—what they did about the problem and what more they would have done if they could have. The principal of a school in which this project was done placed copies of one of the books in the school's library and in her office. She required students who teased their Mountain peers to read it. She stated that once she understood why the teasing occurred, her strategy changed from punishment to education.
9. A mural illustrating Mountain people of courage and accomplishment who lead positive resistance or contribute to human advancement in the arts and sciences.
10. Performance art in which students make or collect slides of the hillbilly image and write a piece that educates while it entertains.
11. A gallery installation in which students display hillbilly images and literature. The installation includes students' responses in the forms of self-portraits, murals, sculptures, and quilts. At the opening of the event, students present a forum for deconstructing popular media portrayals of Mountain Culture.

Critically examining Mountain Culture—the history, resistance, struggles, and productivity of the people—can create respect for identity and pride of place, whether one is a member of that culture or not. Grounding in their cultures keeps young people from internalizing stereotypes and rejecting their traditions. Cultural grounding does not glorify. It promotes a realistic, inclusive view and encourages understanding of other groups. Always the step after establishing pride in oneself and one's culture is studying other cultures that endure stereotyping.

Students who do this can learn to see globally, to recognize their own prejudices, and to discover the universality of their experiences. These may be among our highest goals for education.

NOTES

[1]Approximately 150,000 mining jobs were lost, as were jobs in railroading and related industries. During a ten-year period, more than 650,000 people left the mountains in search of work. Migration from the Appalachian region created pockets of Mountain Cultural communities throughout the United States. The exodus has continued in the past five years for the same reasons, but the numbers are not available.

[2]I collected the following stories from 1995 to 1998 while I attended Appalachian conferences and visited schools.

[3]One book I recommend is *O, Appalachia* by R. Lampell and M. Lampell (1989).

REFERENCES

Bice, D. (1995). *West Virginia and the Appalachian.* Marceline, MO: Walsworth.

Churchill, W. (1996). *Indians are us.* Monroe, ME: Common Courage.

Cunningham, R. (1987). *Apples on the flood.* Knoxville: University of Tennessee Press.

Giroux, H. A. (1993). *Border crossings: Cultural workers and the politics of education.* New York: Routledge, Chapman, and Hall.

Green, A. (1965). Hillbilly music: Source and symbol. *Journal of American Folklore, 78* (309), 204–228.

Hart, L. (1992–1993). The role of cultural context in multicultural aesthetics. *Journal of Multicultural and Cross-cultural Research in Art Education, 10-11,* 5–19.

hooks, b. (1992). Representing whiteness in the black imagination. In L. Grossberg, C. Nelson, & P. Treichler, eds., *Cultural studies* (pp. 330–341). New York: Routledge.

Lampell, R., & M. Lampell. (1989). *O, Appalachia.* New York: Stewart, Tabori & Chang.

Lazar Group. (1995). *Museographs folio* (visuals). Available from Museographs, Lawrenceville, GA.

Morris, C. B. (1997a). A Mountain Cultural curriculum: Telling our story. *Journal of Social Theory in Art Education,* (17) 98–116.

————. (1997b). Seminal seeds and hybrids: Colonialism and Mountain Cultural arts in West Virginia. *Journal of Multicultural and Cross-cultural Research in Art Education* (14), 66–79.

Nakashima, J., producer and director. (1995). *Mountaineers* (film). Available from West Virginia University Public Television, Morgantown.

Price, R. (1998). Funding-suit namesake still fighting for schools. *Columbus Dispatch,* 17 May, p. 1A.

Smith, H. E., producer and director. (1983). *Strangers and kin* (film). Available from Appalshop, Whitesburg, KY.

Wigginton, E. (1972). *The foxfire book.* New York: Doubleday.

Young, J., producer and director. (1994). *Dancin' outlaw* (film). Available from West Virginia University Public Television, Morgantown.

CHAPTER 8

You Don't Need a Penis to Be a Genius

DEBORAH SMITH-SHANK

"You Don't Have to Have a Penis to Be a Genius" is the title of a chapter in Suzi Gablik's (1995) book, *Conversations Before the End of Time*. The title, according to Gablik, comes from one of the early posters designed by the Guerrilla Girls, a group of anonymous women who appeared in 1985 as a gorilla-costumed, trouble-making, media-oriented force to be reckoned with. The Guerrilla Girls stage demonstrations and use sloganed posters to make people aware of the problems that continue to plague women within a gender-unfriendly contemporary art world. Most recently they published a book, *The Guerrilla Girls' Bedside Companion to the History of Western Art* (1998), which is not only informative but also fun to read.

The Guerrilla Girls' penis/genius slogan got your attention, didn't it? It is useful because it is in-your-face. It demands attention, discussion, and contemplation. It irreverently solicits our ideas and comments. When my twenty-year-old daughter discovered a version of this paper on the dining room table, she read the title and moaned, "Oh, Mom! Not again. Can't you stop with the political stuff?" My answer was to remind her about her own experience the previous week, when she (a computer science major) and her boyfriend were shopping for computer hardware. Although my daughter asked the questions, the sales clerk addressed his answers to her boyfriend. I reminded her about how angry she had been, and she relented. This incident illustrates the need for in-your-face confrontations that can lead to discussion, reflection, and, eventually, a more gender-friendly culture.

THE NATURE OF GENIUS

Victoria Neufeldt and David Guralnik (1988) write that *Webster's New World College Dictionary* tells us that the concept of genius comes from an ancient Roman belief that a guardian spirit is assigned to a person at birth and has strong influence over that person's destiny. *Webster's* goes on to define the person of genius as one who has "great mental capacity and inventive ability" and "popularly, any person with a very high intelligence quotient." *Webster's* attributes no sex linkage. However, when I ask my students to list the names of geniuses, they list men such as Einstein, Picasso, Steven Hawking, and even Charles Schulz. Not once in more than three years have they listed a woman.

Catherine Soussloff (1997) and Marybeth Koos (1998) trace the idea of genius through history and explain why it has traditionally been linked with maleness. Theorists linked genius to seminal fluid, which they also linked to creation. Women's bodies were mere flowerpots—containers of damp, moist earth into which men planted their seeds. Gemant (1961), in a thoughtful work titled *The Nature of the Genius,* explained that although some women seem to be smart, a rational explanation clarifies this. Most gifted women aren't really women. "Eminent women scientists are nearly always plain or have definitely masculine features. They are actually half men, physically and mentally, their primary sexual organs happening to be female" (pp. 114–115). Karen Horney (1967) observes, "Scarcely any character trait in woman . . . is not assumed to have an essential root in penis-envy" (p. 247).

Women don't envy penises; women envy access to knowledge and the opportunities knowledge creates. Women have fought throughout history for access to art educations and careers. Many women, including Mary Cassatt and Harriet Hosmer, had to leave the United States to pursue their art educations in other countries. "Heroines have fought harder for knowledge than they have ever fought for love and lovers over the ages. . . . Eve was expelled, as was Pandora, from the Garden of Eden because she sought knowledge forbidden to woman, but granted to man for no other reason than his sex" (Goodrich, 1993, p. xix).

Women still take risks to become artists. According to the Guerrilla Girls (1998), women artists are collected and exhibited less, and the prices of their work are almost never as high as those of males, particularly white males. And statistics indicate that women art teachers receive tenure less often than their male counterparts, and that their salaries are lower (p. 90).

Linda Nochlin (1988), in her landmark article, "Why Have There Been No Great Women Artists?" also considers the question of genius and talent. She cites male historians and biologists who "scientifically" demonstrate "the inability of human beings with wombs rather than penises to create anything significant" (p. 147). Even Mary Cassatt and Georgia O'Keeffe were absent from our childhood schoolbooks and the art history texts of our professional educations. "Women's intellectual [and artistic] contributions were not just forgotten but were actively suppressed" (Seigfried, 1996, p. 23).

Women artists have been erased from our histories, but since the 1960s a number have become known through the recovery efforts of feminist art historians who have introduced us to women of genius such as Artemisia Gentileschi, Rosa Bonheur, and Gertrude Stein. Even when established and powerful men have "killed authors and have burned their books, the only thing needed was a single copy that survived in somebody's pocket, or in somebody's memory, in order to keep the stories alive" (Goodrich, 1993, p. xxvii).

By including women artists whose work was attributed to males (for example, Judith Leyster, in Chadwick, 1990, p. 20), and reminding us of artists such as Sofonisba Anguissola, the content of contemporary art history textbooks has improved. However, placing women of genius and talent into the art education curriculum remains difficult. Although curricular exemplars have become more gender balanced, women artists are still taught far less often than men. (Aren't we all a little tired of hearing only about Cassatt, O'Keeffe, and Kahlo?) Contemporary culture still links talent, genius, and even competence with men (as my daughter's computer store anecdote illustrates). This discussion illuminates the difficulty of transforming ingrained attitudes about genius; however, attitudes can be transformed.

THE TEST OF TIME

Recently I presented a slide lecture at a conference on the HIStorical nature of genius. As I spoke, I introduced a number of women artists. An art teacher/doctoral student in the audience challenged my HERstory with the patented patriarchal comment, "Well, if they haven't stood the test of time, then they probably weren't as good as the men." My response, which included the location of power within the art world, prompted her to rethink her position, but with difficulty. At first she countered with the modernist and time-honored argument about the content of women's artwork. She parroted the criticism that women artists who make personal statements through their artwork are not artists because they are not responding to the universals of significant form. They are "showing off," or they have such small imaginations that they cannot think beyond their own bodies and experiences. She insisted that Art was not craft, and that BIG was better than small. She had been carefully taught.

This woman was actually a thoughtful critic of my presentation. She had learned what her culture and her education had taught her. She is not unlike many of my students, male and female. When students enter my classroom for their first art education methods class, they bring with them considerable cultural baggage, some of which is junk, but not all. Each of my students has had unique and rich experiences. However, many also are loaded down with preconceptions and beliefs that stifle their curiosity, inhibit their exploration, and bind them to stunted ideologies. Much of their cargo has to do with gender and race. When unpacked, this cargo sometimes enriches our conversations. Other times it makes us uncomfortable. When challenged, it may be difficult to reconsider.

American philosopher Charles Sanders Peirce reminds us that "the primary function of thought is the production of belief. And the purpose of belief is to secure new habits that can put thought to rest" (Corrington, 1993, p. 36). As teachers we must create safe climates before discussing gender and race so that our students, rather than unthinkingly defending their ideas, feel free to become uncomfortable with misogyny and racism. Learning happens when students become so uncomfortable with old beliefs that they move to new, more comfortable beliefs.

FEMINIST ART CRITICISM AND BOUNDARIES

Feminism is a word that elicits unreflected beliefs and impassioned responses. Agreeing on a definition is difficult. Since feminism is a living ideology, many varieties exist, and one feminist's feminism may not be another's. Generally, feminism involves the beliefs that gender inequities exist within cultures and that reducing these inequities is possible.

Feminist artwork criticizes existing social orders. It includes expressive forms that go beyond traditional definitions. It sometimes questions art's boundaries. Some feminist artists make disconcerting images about uncomfortable issues. Teachers may wish to discuss these works beyond their formal qualities—what, when, how, and why—and at times extend the discussion beyond the works themselves. Some of my art education students have never discussed art until college, much less had their assumptions challenged by provocative images. Meanings and contexts are important in conversation about art. Both boys and girls can learn that art can be about aging, racism, reproductive rights, motherhood, physical and sexual abuse, standards of beauty, and language as a tool of social control (Tucker & Tanner, 1994, p. 18). These issues are rarely addressed in art classes. Including work by historical and contemporary women artists can remedy this.

Feminist issues are not for women only, and for that matter both genders benefit from considering male body images too. Claes Oldenburg's *Bat Column,* which looms in downtown Chicago, comes to mind.

HEROINES

We all need heroines. In college no painter role models were like me. My professors did not discuss women artists. I didn't know of any women painters (dead or alive), and I had no women professors in studio art. My hero was Picasso, and I wanted to be just like him (see Smith-Shank, 1998). For years I didn't realize that being like Picasso wasn't what I wanted, or that he was not a role model for a budding feminist. I did have many women role models in art education, and I value their influence, but I could have used a studio-oriented heroine too.

In a book aptly titled *Heroines,* Norma Goodrich (1993) gives us the character traits of a true heroine: she must have demonstrated an admirable personality, triumphed over danger, proved herself fearless against strictures she judged unfair, scorned blind fortune and hostile gods, and acted well when called on with a cool head and a firm step (p. xxiii).

This description caused me to reflect on women artists I know. All fit this description. Our male and female students must learn of hidden-stream artists who lovingly embellish their homes with quilts, clothing, weaving, and pottery, of mainstream women artists who found their voices, and of deceased women artists who have been rediscovered. Unless these issues are addressed in art education, they will never be addressed for most people.

My encounters with patriarchy always surprise me. I was surprised by my daughter's experience in the computer store, despite its ordinariness. Such encounters need to become uncomfortably extraordinary. Studying feminist art first teaches our students that discrimination

against women still exists. Then it encourages them to question their assumptions about notions such as the link between gender and genius. Finally, it guides them in replacing old sexist habits.

FINAL THOUGHTS

When I first considered writing this chapter, I planned to include the
word *feminist* in the title to cue readers to the content and ensure a safe,
self-selecting audience. However, after I started, I decided an in-your-
face approach was better despite the possibility that such a title on my
Faculty Service Report will not impress my dean. Well, I concluded, I'm
tired of preaching to the choir. A colleague suggested that if one associ-
ates with company whose behavior is more radical than one's own, then
one's own radicalism may appear mild. If so, perhaps linking my chapter
title to the Guerrilla Girls will save me.

I consider the Guerrilla Girls heroines, and I support their calls to
arms. They inspire me to respond to my daughter's question, "Can't you
stop with the political stuff?" by answering, "I'm sorry, Bridget, but not
yet."

What would Western art history be without Gentileschi, Bonheur,
Lewis, Kahlo, or any of the women who are or would have been in this
book? What would contemporary art be without all the great women
artists of the past few decades? Let's make sure the work of women and
artists of color is valued, exhibited, and preserved by our institutions.
The Guerrilla Girls plan to continue pressuring the art world. "We'll continue to identify and ridicule the powers that be and to drag the misogy-
nists and racists kicking and screaming into the 21st century. We invite
you to join us. Tell your local galleries and museums how to behave.
Write letters, make posters, make trouble" (Guerrilla Girls, 1998, p. 91).

Teachers must ensure that all students learn about male AND female
artists of genius. We must nurture the guardian spirit of creativity that is
found equally within both genders.

REFERENCES

Chadwick, W. (1990). *Women, art, and society.* London: Thames and Hudson.
Corrington, R. S. (1993). *An introduction to C. S. Peirce: Philosopher, semioti-
cian, and esthetic naturalist.* Lanham, MD: Rowman & Littlefield.
Gablik, S. (1995). *Conversations before the end of time.* New York: Thames and
Hudson.

Gemant, A. (1961). *The nature of the genius.* Springfield, IL: Charles C Thomas.

Goodrich, N. L. (1993). *Heroines.* New York: HarperCollins.

The Guerrilla Girls. (1998). *The Guerrilla Girls' bedside companion to the history of Western art.* New York: Penguin.

Horney, K. (1967). *Feminine psychology.* New York: Norton.

Koos, M. (1998). The genius in time. Paper presented at the meeting of the American Educational Research Association, San Diego, CA.

Neufeldt, V., & Guralnik, D., eds. (1998). *Webster's new world college dictionary.* New York: Macmillan.

Nochlin, L. (1988). Why have there been no great women artists? In *Women, art, and power and other essays* (pp. 145–176). New York: Harper & Row.

Seigfried, C. (1996). *Pragmatism and feminism: Reviewing the social fabric.* Chicago: University of Chicago Press.

Smith-Shank, D. (1998). Sugar and spice and everything: Reflections on a feminist aesthetic. *Journal of Social Theory in Art Education, 18,* 21–28.

Soussloff, C. M. (1997). *The absolute artist: The historiography of a concept.* Minneapolis: University of Minnesota Press.

Tucker, M., & Tanner, M. (1994). *Bad girls.* New York: New Museum of Contemporary Art.

Real-World Art Lessons: Ignoring the Rules

KRIS FEHR

The authors in Part III teach outside the rules. Where others say, "You can't do that," they emphatically say, "Oh yes, we can." And they tell us how we can too. They take on controversial issues, which is courageous in a conservative field. Whether the rules are real or imagined, we often fear teaching something that seems too political, too sensitive, too impossible. When these authors take a stand, they are passionate about their ideas and clear about their arguments. They understand the political nature of education and how to work within it. Part III helps us evaluate what we are teaching. It shows us how to ignore the rules.

Part III opens with "Investigating the Culture of Curriculum." Olivia Gude compares current art world issues with today's school art curricula. She finds them sadly unrelated. She suggests that much school art conveys dated definitions of art. She calls for teachers to redefine today's art curricular foundations by using an approach that draws on hidden, missing, and contextualized curricula.

In "Art in the Dark: A Nonvisual Learners' Curriculum," Lisette Ewing describes a curriculum she developed for visual and nonvisual learners. She goes beyond including visually impaired students in studio activities by including them in viewing as well. This is no Working with Clay 101—students combine textures and found objects to create projects they then critique and exhibit publicly. Ewing recommends the curriculum even for classes comprising only visual learners because it can broaden their definitions of art.

In "Tough School Teaching: Myths of Creation and Destruction," Frank Pio shows us how he taught students to make culture-affirming art in one of the most challenging school settings imaginable. We watch Pio transform from a teacher who fails to resolve a racially based fistfight with talk of love and friendship to one who develops an ambitious mural project that results in racial healing.

Pio's project incorporates the creation and destruction myths of many cultures, but as Future Akins points out in "Simply Sacred," the sacred as a source of creative power is seldom discussed in classrooms. Building on Parker Palmer's definition of the sacred as that which we hold with respect, she discusses how teachers can bring the sacred into their classrooms by respecting self, place, and others. She writes that when we allow students to help with planning their curriculum, we define art as "a self-motivated process expressing what is important to each of us."

Mary Wyrick deconstructs the media's one-dimensional portrayal of women in "Identity, Sexuality, and Power: Art and the Media." She describes how the work of several politically driven artists motivated her university art education students to develop lessons that teach young people to identify inconsistencies between media messages and the realities of their lives.

In "Sexual Identity in the Art Room," Laurel Lampela makes a case for discussing artists' sexual identities in art class. She differentiates between discussing sexual identities and discussing the intimate details of artists' sex lives, a distinction lost on some critics. She explains how knowledge of artists' sexual identities can help viewers understand their work. More important, when we mention artists' sexual identities, we are saying our classrooms are places of safety and respect.

CHAPTER 9

Investigating the Culture of Curriculum

OLIVIA GUDE

I recently asked prospective teachers in my Foundations of Art Education course to list visual art topics that they found important. Their list included urban architecture, controversial art, the legitimacy of making art from pop culture imagery, the possibility of universal values in art, feminist art, altar making for holidays such as *Dia de los Muertos,* outsider or folk art, and alternative comic books.

A few weeks later, without referring to our earlier exercise, I asked the students to list curriculum topics for a high school art course. Their list included the elements and principles of design, printmaking, color mixing, painting, figure drawing, computer art, impressionism, surrealism, and pop art.

Although I had expected differences between what was perceived as important and what was perceived as being appropriate for a high school course, I was surprised at the degree of disparity between the lists. The first list included some of the most important art issues in today's world; most of the issues on the second list would have been appropriate seventy-five years ago, or more important art historically. These students visualized the curriculum as a recycled version of their own public school art experiences rather than as an engagement with the politics of contemporary visual culture. What could account for the failure of these emerging teachers to imagine a current approach to art education?

HOW FIRM ARE THE FOUNDATIONS
OF ART EDUCATION?

Certain art exercises so typify art education since at least mid-twentieth-century that they may appear to be perpetually appropriate. However, art's many histories and theoretical layers, the influence of technology on meaning, new ideas about production and perception, contemporary notions of artistic integrity, changing responsibilities between the artist and society, and new definitions of visual research make clear that yesterday's wisdom may be today's folly.

Recently I viewed images by students who attended the Bauhaus, an institution that shaped modernist aesthetics in the 1920s and 1930s. The students' projects resembled the work of noted Bauhaus artists and other important figures of the time. For example, a student exercise exploring qualities of line was similar to Paul Klee's drawings, and an exercise based on squares looked similar to works by Piet Mondrian.

These are not examples of masters inappropriately influencing pupils, but rather examples from a good learning situation in which projects were designed to help students explore the latest thinking in art. It made sense *then* to concentrate on the formal properties of art making because these properties were one of the important aspects of these artists' work. I found similar congruencies within other artistic traditions. In each, a fit was achieved linking the art of the time, the contemporary aesthetic theories underlying it, and the teaching that introduced students to it.

Age alone does not render instructional approaches obsolete. Much art of the past speaks to us today, and traditional art exercises may be useful in understanding it. However, students today often complete school art programs that ignore postmodern art and even a great deal of modern art. Curricula that stress art history that ends with cubism; visual elements and principles; and color wheels, technical skills, and other aspects of art production are already over half a century out-of-date. This approach is comparable to teaching science with no mention of space travel.

What do students thus trained miss in, say, Miriam Schapiro's fabric paintings or Andy Goldsworthy's environmental sculptures? Schapiro's provocative cultural dialogue about how societies create and value gender roles. Goldsworthy's probing commentaries on humanity's relationship to an increasingly fragile world. The main course, in other words. These students are left to nurture their aesthetic selves on the NutraSweet

their training in formal analysis allows—appreciation of the visual qualities of the work.

When planning an art curriculum, a teacher might ask, "Since this
may be THE LAST ART CLASS my students will take, what do they
need to know to begin a meaningful lifelong engagement with art?"
Ruthlessly examine projects already in the curriculum. Sometimes we
are so comfortable with old projects that it is hard to see that they may
have lost their relevance. Ask: Does this lesson teach a dated view of art?
Does this content justify the time spent on it? Is a week spent on a value
scale wise? The rationale that students are polishing their ruler and brush
control skills sounds . . . well, pathetic.

This is not to say that skill-level knowledge is unimportant. However, we must recognize that such knowledge is not foundational; it is not
needed before issues of contemporary art and culture are introduced.

The next question is: Then what is foundational today? One answer
takes the form of a consistent theme in postmodern discourse: Nothing
can be considered foundational for all cases. Is all then lost? No. Contemporary teachers choose what is foundational for their specific teaching settings. They observe what others suggest and then have the
confidence to decide for themselves, acknowledging their own uncertainties in their curricula. They understand that introducing students to
current and at times controversial cultural debates will not harm them,
but rather will give them the tools to be thoughtful visual citizens.

INVESTIGATING THE CULTURE OF CURRICULUM

One notion that some may find foundational is investigation. Create curricula that encourage students to investigate questions linking visual and
social issues. Many interesting art projects mimic our best contemporary
art in that both encourage reconsideration of "the real," "the natural,"
and "the normal"—and recognition that these concepts are socially
constructed.

In a program on contemporary art called the Spiral Workshop at the
University of Illinois in Chicago, my colleagues and I develop art curricula for high schools and middle schools. The goal is not to come up with
a new orthodoxy, a single set of projects or ideas that sum up the totality
of today's art discourses, but rather to disrupt traditional means of thinking about culture and art. Ours is an eclectic, postmodern approach to
curriculum construction—pick through curriculum artifacts, refurbish

what is still useful, discard what is not, and introduce new content when needed.

Investigating the culture of curriculum can start with three areas—contextualized curriculum, hidden curriculum, and missing curriculum. In this chapter I discuss the concepts of context and absence for curricula development and then describe two art lessons that include personal relevancy, contemporary social themes, a study of artworks related to the theme, and art making.

CONTEXTUALIZING DECONTEXTUALIZED CURRICULA

Two effective ways to revitalize your curriculum are to contextualize it historically and to rationalize your reasons for choosing it. For example, if you teach linear perspective, you might inform the students that it was developed to represent a three-dimensional view of the world as perceived by Europeans of the fifteenth century. Telling students that perspective was developed by a particular culture at a particular time can raise useful questions: Is this the best way to represent space? What means have other cultures derived? Is one means better than another? Teachers cannot answer these questions adequately without a pancultural range of exemplars that may include Ancient Egypt, China, South Central Asia, Modernist Europe and Mexico, and folk and outsider art. Then of course there are the cultures that developed no method—why? The class might even investigate whether a correlation exists between a culture's acceptance of an unvarying aesthetic viewpoint and its ability to understand the viewpoints of others.

Note how contextualizing a skill-level lesson on technique led to a learning experience about multiple points of view that spans continents and centuries and creates an authentic cross-cultural awareness of non-Western ways of seeing and knowing. How different from multicultural education as a charming aside to the main menu of Renaissance illusionism. Here, other means of representation were validated, and students became free from the obsession that technological exactitude is a precondition for good artistry.

METAMESSAGES IN THE HIDDEN CURRICULUM

The term *hidden curriculum* refers to the transmittal of knowledge without conscious intent. An example of a hidden art curriculum would be our linear perspective lesson had it not been contextualized. In this case, a portrayal of progress, achievement, and a universal applicability of Western art forms may convey a tacit message of cultural superiority. Failure to portray non-Western views would convey a second message— that they are unworthy. A cavalier portrayal conveys a similar message— they are worthy only as diversions.

Another example of a hidden art world curriculum was articulated by pioneers of the women's movement in the 1970s. Classic essays such as Linda Nochlin's (1971) "Why Have There Been No Great Women Artists?" drew attention to the absence of women artists in art history courses and museums.

Art as a product of individual genius is another assumption conveyed by the hidden curriculum. Even art programs that include women and people of color may teach that great art is the product of great individuals, rather than a kind of cultural production involving complex social interactions among numbers of people.

Despite a vast heritage of art created by collective design and execution, the art taught in our schools implies that objects of sole authorship are most worth teaching. Few programs include the study of collaborative art making. Students do not learn the ego-releasing pleasure of techniques such as the surrealist Exquisite Corpse or dadaist chance poetry. Students do not make collaborative public projects in the manner of the community mural movement. Students do not learn of contemporary intergenerational collaborations such as the stylish conceptual paintings of Tim Rollins and his Kids of Survival (Gablik, 1992).

In a culture whose social fabric appears threatened by individualism and a breakdown of community, many art education curricula teach students to work silently and alone, making individual projects that will eventually be thrown away. Perhaps here we see another unintended message emerging in the hidden curriculum—the marginality and uselessness of art today.

The missing curriculum is closely related to the hidden curriculum. Scrutiny of the hidden curriculum often points to underrepresented artists and ideas. The missing curriculum points to social issues related to visual culture that merit investigation within an art program.

PROJECTS

At Spiral Workshop we consider four components when designing a project. Each project should (1) deal with an issue important to students,

(2) be based on a contemporary social theme, (3) include examples of past and recent artworks that have explored the theme, and (4) teach a method (conceptual and/or technical) for constructing works of art.

Project One: Problematized Body Sculptures

Hated Body Parts is a sculpture project developed because we recognized that, although self-portraiture and drawing the human figure are both included in most art curricula, the two are seldom joined. Students often portray their faces but almost never their bodies. Relentless media attention to dieting and eating disorders suggests that the body is an important concern in contemporary culture. Body image is a major issue for many teens, and much contemporary art challenges the naturalness of today's standards of physical beauty.

To complete this project, the students chose body parts about which they had obsessed or felt special concern. After drawing and writing about these parts of their bodies, the students created plaster carvings of their "problem areas"—an amusing variation of the tradition of copying "perfect" body parts. The resulting sculptures gave interesting insights into how students related to their own bodies. Many pieces were funny, some ironic, and some quite poignant. The final piece was a collaborative installation of bas-relief sculptures and texts in which students created a safe space to discuss feelings about their bodies.

Project Two: Image Banks and Desire

Symbolic self-portrait collages made from a randomly collected selection of magazines is a common art project. It may be more educational to have students first analyze the goals of the magazines available and then say, "Choose from this highly preselected bank of images."

I suggest that a comprehensive art education includes study of our increasingly image-based consumer culture. Yet a bigger taboo in the schools than nudity or eroticism is how these images turn human beings into consumers by turning everyday goods (soap, shoes, stoves, cars) into objects of desire. Spiral Workshop created a project appropriately called Stuff, which encourages students to explore their relationship to consumer desire.

Students search magazines, cutting out images of things they want. Then we ask them to think about how they use things to construct idealized versions of themselves. They fill out worksheets with stories of pleasure, desire, and disappointment: "List three things you have wanted but never received. List something you wanted, then received, then disliked."

Students enjoy discussing past clothing and toy fads—things they wanted "way back then" that seem silly and useless now. Such discussions give them perspective on the socially constructed nature of their desires. As the project evolves, students combine tracings and photographs of things with text and images of themselves—a self-portrait exploring how their identities are interwoven with possession. The purpose of this project is not to condemn material pleasure but to encourage students to explore questions of identity and compare how their definitions may differ from those of people in other times and places.

EVALUATING YOUR ART CURRICULUM

If you wish to reconsider your current curriculum, try to see how it portrays the world. If this portrayal is not as complex and contradictory as the world itself, then analyze, edit, contextualize, and invent fresh curricular approaches. While professors and politicians wrangle about who should be included in the canon and what should be taught in our schools, art teachers can quietly and competently teach curricula that subvert cultural and corporate control.

REFERENCES

Gablik, S. (1992). *The reenchantment of art.* London: Thames and Hudson.

Nochlin, L. (1971). Why have there been no great women artists? In T. Hess & E. Baker, eds., *Art and sexual politics* (pp. 1–44). New York: Collier. Originally published in *ARTnews,* January 1971, pp. 22–39, 67–71.

CHAPTER 10

Art in the Dark: A Nonvisual Learners' Curriculum

LISETTE EWING

This chapter is for people who believe art should be taught to everyone. Specifically, it is a guide for teachers who want to teach art to blind and visually impaired students or, as I will call them, nonvisual learners. First I relate how my interest in teaching art to nonvisual learners evolved. Then I describe Art in the Dark, a project I developed to accomplish this. Last, I address general considerations for teachers who wish to incorporate Art in the Dark into their curricula.

As a child I loved art. I eagerly anticipated my art teachers' visits and my classroom teachers' art lessons. My parents were artistic as well. I remember my mother's oil paintings (done in our laundry room) and my father's drawings and photographs.

I remember taking art lessons from an elderly woman in our neighborhood. When I recall these lessons, the individual projects do not stand out in my mind. I remember the smells from her kitchen as I walked to the staircase leading to her loft and the sound of her European accent as she taught me about art. My childhood art education was multisensory.

As a college student studying education for nonvisual learners, I noticed that art was omitted from the curriculum. When I questioned this, my professors told me these students needed to learn Braille, abacus, money identification, dollar-bill folding, slate and stylus, Nemeth code Braille for math and science, typing, writing on raised-line paper, travel orientation and mobility, word processing, Web browsing with screen readers and refreshable and computerized Braille translation. There was no room for art, since nonvisual learners couldn't do much with it anyway.

I did not accept that experts in my field made room for music, the-ater, and dance but not art. As a student teacher I taught myself how to teach art to nonvisual learners. We did "touch pictures" by attaching rub-ber bands, shredded corks, crinkle foil, and wax paper to surfaces. We did color studies in terms of language and texture. How do we know blue is cold and orange is warm?

What did I find? That my nonvisual students loved art. They wanted to do and know more.

"What are the different kinds of art?"

"Where is art?"

"What artists are famous?"

"Can we be artists?"

THE QUESTIONNAIRE

After graduating I became an itinerant teacher of mainstreamed nonvi-sual students and moved into the next step of my mission: talking with art teachers about teaching nonvisual learners. I designed and sent a questionnaire to the art teachers in my school district. I also designed and sent a questionnaire to my district's nonvisual students. I received re-sponses from six students.

The results from the art teachers were as I had hoped. Ninety-three percent felt that art was "very important" to blind children's develop-ment. When asked about their comfort with teaching art to blind stu-dents, 60 percent stated that they would feel comfortable. When asked how much support they would need from the itinerant teacher, 85 percent stated "very much." These data suggested that most art teachers were eager to integrate nonvisual learners if specialists would assist them.

Six students—three in elementary school, one in middle school, and two in high school—responded to the questionnaires. All studied art in elementary school. The three older students all studied art in middle school. Neither of the oldest students studied art in high school. One respondent indicated out-of-school art activity. When asked how they de-fined art, three chose "sculptures and paintings," and three chose "activ-ity of creating beautiful things." Three had been to tactile displays in art museums. The survey suggested that art is part of some nonvisual learn-ers' educations but generally less so than with sighted learners.

THE PROJECT

The questionnaire inspired me to study art education within a master's program (Ewing, 1991). My goal was to blend my expertise with nonvisual learners with my art education and apply it in a school setting.

For my thesis I developed Art in the Dark, a curriculum for teaching tactually oriented art to high school classes. I used the art teacher's curriculum and the *4J School District Visual Arts Council Position Paper* (1990), which provides these guidelines: "Students and teachers need to recognize that the need goes beyond art production activities by expanding into the additional content areas of contemporary art and social issues, art history, art criticism, and aesthetics. It is critical that we recognize the importance of teaching students about art as well as about how to make art" (p. A42).

Since the 1975 passage of Public Law 94-142 art classes commonly include students with physical, mental, and learning differences. The Art in the Dark project consisted of three weeks of study involving exploration, production, lecture, critique, and exhibition during which nonsighted and sighted students learned from one another.

Nonvisual learners are defined as those with visual acuity of less than 20/200. To experience art nonvisually, the sighted students made eye coverings that impaired their vision by covering ski goggles or safety glasses with spray paint, rubber cement, or tape. This method was preferable to blindfolds because it allowed normal eye movement.

The students began with quick assignments to grow accustomed to working without sight. They progressed gradually to final pieces intended for exhibition.

THE EXHIBITION

In 1934 John Dewey expressed a challenge answered by Art in the Dark: "When artistic objects are separated from both conditions of origin and operation in experience, a wall is built around them that renders almost opaque their general significance" (p. 3). If a nonvisual student creates a work of art, the work must be perceived tactually.

The exhibit was titled *Get a Feel for Art*. Some of the work was displayed under boxes with hand holes cut out. Tactile art can also be displayed behind vertical blinds through which people reach. The students placed their goggles for visitors in accessible places throughout the exhibit, and volunteers guided viewers who wore them. Please Touch signs cued visitors, and the students instructed them as well.

GENERAL CONSIDERATIONS

Environment and Materials

The art room can be a place to learn self-esteem, independence, problem solving, and communicative skills in addition to art. To encourage this with nonvisual learners, the environment does not need to be neat, but it needs to be organized. Nonvisual students must know where to find things.

Conventional art room materials are not always appropriate. We used wire, fabric, electronic parts, scrap metal, plastics, parts of toys, pieces of hardware, foil, leather, wood, yarn, and other found objects.

Teamwork

Integrating students with special needs calls for a team of adults and an Individual Education Plan (IEP) for each special needs student. A specialist most likely will be available. Placing art goals on IEPs can be a way to involve a specialist in your classroom. The specialist can assist with room mobility, labeling with large print or Braille, art materials, and approaches that work with a specific student.

Language

I suggest that art is more than visual perception. One of my teaching strategies was to "talk and talk and talk" while the students worked. I rarely allowed the radio. This strategy aids nonvisual learners and prompts both kinds of learners to consider social and ethical issues, aesthetics, the media, technology, and history. Invite students to comment and question.

Nonvisual learners may have some vision. Never be afraid to ask students what works best for them. Expressions such as *look* and *see* are fine. Avoid *over there* or *right here*. The more descriptive the language, the better. Teach your visual learners to speak descriptively. This benefits both kinds of learners as they enhance their language with rich visual descriptions.

Experimentation

Welcome to the class where anything goes and everything is new. Throw your expectations about outcomes out the window. Place your emphasis on process. Art in the Dark is an ongoing exploration of materials. At one point we explored metaphorical differences in meaning between cut and whole rubber bands.

One aspect of teaching sighted students that is equally effective for nonvisual students is periodic exposure to one another's work in progress. Ask students to discuss what is working and not working for them. Tactile exploration of various solutions also encourages discussion about aesthetic values, creativity, and visual metaphors.

Critiques

For Art in the Dark critiques, students, goggles on, sit around a table. The first student describes his or her work as the class passes the work around. The following conversation describes how my group wrestled with how to title a work of art.

"It's all grassy feeling and wire. There's fuzzy stuff here and poky stuff over here."

"This is kinda weird, funny stuff. Really *weird*. It makes noise."

"It's rubbery, stringy. It looks like egg whites."

"I'd title it *Awkward* because it's different looking."

"Feels like a mound of trash. I'd call it *Top of the Heap*."

"It feels like pine needles and moss. I'd call it *Forest Floor*."

"Feels like stir-fry."

"I'd call it *Weary* because it's all bunched up and scattered."

Even without sight, students may use expressions such as *looks like* as they translate tactile qualities into inner visualizations. Interpreting textures as means of artistic expression can enhance all interpretative inquiry. Discussing differences in students' interpretations can reveal as much about their worldviews as about art objects.

The comments below are from a student who particularly enjoyed Art in the Dark. She titled her piece *White-Collar World at a High-Rise Price*:

I wanted to portray the coldness of the white-collar world. The raised part is supposed to be a building. The base is big, off the table. Fabric covers the base, cotton, which is what all the businessmen wear. The sides are tucked so it's nice and neat. The metal is to represent cold. The box on it represents packaging. The business world is always fast paced. Feel the ridges on this round thing? That represents time. That's what the knobs here are for. Feel how fast paced it is?

For integration to be successful, teachers must be comfortable with innovation. Not only students with special needs, but the entire group, must adapt.

Evaluation

The students answered evaluative questions at the end of the project. Selected answers follow.

How do you describe creating art with altered vision?

"It's fun . . . The actual art of it is the way it feels . . . not what it will look like when you take off your goggles."

Do the elements of design apply to this kind of art?

"Line. It helps create, but you really don't think about the lines when you feel it."

"Texture, curvature, and shape seem more important."

"I think line could be used. Rigidity, feeling, structure."

"Color doesn't really apply because it has too many meanings."

"I think it'd be boring to have sculptures of geometric shapes. They're not interesting enough."

"If you add some lines and texture and different things on it, it'd be more interesting."

Did making art with altered vision benefit you in your visual art?

"Yeah, it makes you get into textures more."

"The art becomes more than just the way it looks."

"If you were blind and wanted to do visual art, it's possible. It's just how you feel things."

Art History

How does one present art images to nonvisual learners? Verbal descriptions work well, especially when more than one person contributes. The more perspectives nonvisual learners hear, the better they can form their perceptions. Nonvisual learners can motivate visual learners to expand their descriptions.

Field trips with hands-on experiences are excellent also. Many art museums will accommodate "touch" experiences if given adequate time to prepare. Art education supply catalogs sell art replicas, and loaner libraries will loan them. Perhaps a local sculptor would love to bring works to your class.

CONCLUSION

Art as human expression transcends the visual. The more accessible art is to visual learners, the more it becomes part of their lives. This is equally true of nonvisual learners. Our field benefits by integrating nonvisual learners into our classrooms. Most art teachers are creative individuals who see this integration as an opportunity to benefit all students.

REFERENCES

Dewey, J. (1934). *Art as experience*. New York: Minton Balch.

Ewing, L. (1991). Integrating an alter-visual learner and tactually oriented art into a visual art course. Manuscript, University of Oregon.

4J School District Visual Arts Council position paper. (1990). Eugene, OR: 4J School District.

FURTHER READING

Dalki, C. (1984). There are no cows here: Art education and special education together at last. *Art Education, 37* (6), 6–9.

Eguren Saez, P. (1989). Integration of blind and visually impaired children: The philosophy. *Journal of Visual Impairment and Blindness, 37* (1), 54–56.

Emmer, J. (1989). Teaching them to see: A non-visual art course. *College Teaching, 37* (1), 21–22.

Fukurai, S. (1974). *How can I make what I cannot see?* New York: Van Nostrand Reinhold.

Lowenfeld, V. (1939). *The nature of creative activity*. London: Routledge and Kegan Paul.

Pazienza, J. (1976). Mainstreaming in art education: A case of the blind leading the blind. *Art Education, 36* (6), 15–17.

Rubin, J. (1976). The exploration of a "tactile aesthetic." *New Outlook, 70* (9), 369–375.

Shore, I. (1989). *Access to art: Art museum directory for blind and visually impaired people*. New York: American Foundation for the Blind and Museum of American Folk Art.

CHAPTER 11

Tough School Teaching: Myths of Creation and Destruction

FRANK PIO

Racial conflict, a major cause of violence, is one of the most troubling problems facing schools today (Barfield, 1995; Devine, 1996; Walker, 1995). Yet inner-city schools are not the hellish places to teach that some believe, if teachers encourage teamwork and understanding of diverse cultures. Such understanding does not occur naturally. In this chapter I describe my experience teaching "tough kids" who initially refused to cross cultural boundaries. Some members of each ethnic group considered their group superior to the others. I believe that social reconstructionist art education can level these hierarchical constructions.

From 1992 to 1996 I worked in a mentor program at New York University's School of Education, through which I was assigned to Seward Park High School (SPHS), an annex on Manhattan's Lower East Side. At Seward Park Annex I worked with students who fit John Devine's (1996) definition of the student at risk: "The student who comes into a building only to cut classes and wander the halls most of the day, playing and roaming as if totally at home in the space but also disrupting classrooms and generally causing havoc" (p. 17).

When I first arrived at the annex, I felt as if I had entered a prison. The campus was drab and run down. During my first two weeks I discovered hostility among Puerto Rican, Mexican, African American, and Asian students. They robbed one another in stairwells while administrators watched through their own racist lenses.

One day I found myself in the middle of a fight. A Chicano student had accused an Asian American student of worshipping multiple gods and eating smelly food. The Asian student responded by accusing him of worshipping voodoo gods and having a smelly body. When the students calmed down, I tried to dispel their misunderstandings in a group discussion by pointing out that they had much in common: the need to be loved, to have friends, to eat, to laugh. I failed.

Bennett Remier and Ralph Smith (1992) suggest that art can encourage teamwork, promote understanding across cultures, and reach students discouraged by racial tension. Working from this assumption, I developed a program intended to heal racial conflict. I decided to base the art curriculum on creation and destruction myths from Latin American, Asian American, African American, and Native American cultures. I established two goals for my students: They would work together making art that involved sharing of their beliefs, and they would learn to respect one another's beliefs.

A MYTH-CENTERED ART CURRICULUM

The myths of a people are born from confrontations with reality. They reflect humanity's need to find meaning. These transgenerational interpretations of reality, although rich with symbolism and subtlety, can be perceived as irrelevant. When concepts of reality change for a cultural group, its myths may appear either dogmatic or superstitious.

I have spent parts of six years as a participant/observer studying the Ojibwe of Ontario, Canada; the Quechua of Peru; and the Hopi and the Zuni of the United States. I have learned that their creation and destruction myths parallel one another as well as those of Judeo-Christianity. I felt that if students discovered these parallels in their cultural myths, they might develop better understandings of their differences.

But how? Multicultural lesson plans of non-Western cultures in Western art curricula often trivialize the Other. I determined to respectfully present the worldviews of different cultures expressed in myths to my students. I used the conceptual model of the Ojibwe medicine wheel to organize content areas of the curriculum. I began to think about ways that it could shape my teaching, and I developed a project that referenced one's place in relation to cardinal directions as metaphors for ways of knowing.

My objectives were to:

1. Develop ethnic pride.
2. Use art and myths to impart cultural understandings.

3. Create murals that would depict a variety of cultural beliefs.
4. Encourage artistic confidence.
5. Motivate students to develop educational goals, verbal skills, and historical perspectives on their sociocultural situations.
6. Enable students to earn two high school credits, one in art and one in English.

Student Selection

I posted program application advertisements throughout the school, and I put flyers into teachers' mailboxes.[1] I based selection on applicants' interest in the program's artistic activities. I did not stipulate a need for prior knowledge or artistic competence. Students ranged in age from fifteen to nineteen, and in grade from nine to twelve. The thirty students who participated in the project over the four years from 1992 to 1996 represented Asian, Native American, Latin American, and African American heritages. No whites were enrolled.

THE OJIBWE MEDICINE WHEEL AS CURRICULAR DESIGN

I used the Ojibwe medicine wheel, illustrated on page 98, to symbolize to my students that they would study nontraditional art content from culturally diverse sources. Starting from this premise, we replaced divisive environmental, racial, and class practices with touchpoints of unity among cultural groups. This project aligns with social theory–based art education.

The Ojibwe believe in circular or cyclical time and that humans, as allies of the environment, play a part in a vast life cycle. From these beliefs the Ojibwe developed their medicine wheel, which they use for healing. The wheel refers to the four cardinal points of direction. Each direction links to a color, an animal, and a set of principles.

I based my four curricular components on the Ojibwe medicine wheel: mythical history, myths as expressions of the philosophies of cultural groups, painting murals, and students as teachers.

History: East/Eagle/Yellow/Beginnings

The art lesson began with Ojibwe mythical history. A historical approach to myth allows students insight into the memories of shared human experiences. According to the Ojibwe, history reveals all the emotions, values, and ideals for which humans live, struggle, and die. Students read and discussed myths of various cultures. Following the discussions, the students visited four museums in Manhattan: the Chinatown History Museum, the Museum of African Art, El Museo del Barrio, and the American Indian Community House Gallery/Museum.

Philosophy: South/Deer/Red/Strength

Next, students explored the philosophies expressed in myths. I explained to the students that philosophy is the ideals of a culture expressed within its art. As a beginning exercise, students created lists that they felt characterized each culture. This exercise revealed a range of stereotypes. For example, one student wrote, "Black people eat watermelon and they're stupid." Another wrote that Asians "are all short and good at math and eat a lot of rice." A third wrote that Native Americans are "stupid, drink a lot, are always drunk, and wear feathers in their hair." One wrote that Latin Americans are "troublemakers."

This exercise established our baseline. We then entered into our study of philosophical principles, which led to the murals themselves.

Art: West/Black Bear/Black/Emotions

Art was the keystone of this myth-centered curriculum. As the students visually interpreted their newly acquired historical and philosophical knowledge, art offered a means to construct their new awareness. Working both in groups and individually, they created proposal drawings for the murals. Then as a group they evaluated their own and one another's work and collectively selected the final composition. At that point I taught them the technical skills that they needed to create the mural.

For the first two years (excluding summers), students met for one ninety-minute period weekly. I worked with a different group of students each year. We worked in my classroom for the first four months, creating the concepts and then the designs for the murals. The remainder of the year students met in the cafeteria, where they painted murals. Drawing and painting each mural took approximately fifty hours.

During the summer months of the third and fourth years, I ran a four-week summer program. Each summer I had a different group of students. We met five hours a day for five days a week. The first summer, the students' mural depicted their version of a creation myth. At the end of each summer session, students presented their work to their peers, teachers, and administrators.

Education: North/White Bear/White/Truth/Knowledge

In the final phase, students became teachers. Students communicated what they learned by creating forums for the school's art classes. The students videotaped and photographed the projects with equipment provided by New York University's Department of Art and Art Professions. The students from the second summer program created a seven-minute video of their project. I gave each student a sketchbook for drawing and note taking at the beginning of the course.

The principal attended the art class presentations. The principal's involvement was important for political and educational reasons: if the program was to continue, the principal's support was needed. To garner the principal's support, he had to be educated. Until he observed the presentations, most student encounters with him were precipitated by disruptive student behavior. This project provided an opportunity for him to observe the students' motivation, discipline, cooperation, and focus.

OUTCOMES

Students over the four years of this program created seven acrylic murals ranging in size from five feet by eight feet to ten feet by twenty feet. Five are in the cafeteria of the annex, and the other two are at SPHS. The cafeteria, one of the few common areas within the annex, was an appropriate meeting ground for sharing cosmic views and facilitating intergroup harmony.[2]

During the courses, students also explored the following questions:

1. *What is a myth?*
   Students came to view myths as stories that communicate major beliefs intergenerationally. One student described myths as "a way of telling a story but only in a more exaggerated way."
2. *What is art?*
   One student came to view art as a "feeling" or "picture" he saw in his mind and tried to put "into your mind by drawing it on a sheet of paper" the way he imagined it.

   Another came to see art "as a way of life. Art is a special way to express your feelings. Everyone knows how to draw. Some people may think they can't draw, but they can. Art is a wonderful way to express the type of person you are."
4. *What is culture?*

One student stated, "Cultures are about people of different races and colors." Early in the course one non-Asian explained why he knew all about Asians: "I see them on the streets, and I have many conversations with Asian Americans, and I see them on TV; therefore, I know all about them."

One student's early description of African Americans was: "Those people are drug pushers." Another student saw Native Americans as "dark people with feathers who live in small houses in the West." Students learned from studying cultural myths that they had held stereotypes fueled by the media, especially TV. The media, they realized, created racial misconceptions and disrespect, and sometimes this led to violent behavior.

5. *What is racism?*

The students shared personal encounters with racism. One described a shopping experience in which the cashier continuously ignored her while serving others. Another described being tormented at school because of her race. She confessed that there were times when the torment made her wish she were dead.

Grading

Students received marks in art and English based on the following criteria, which I explained to them at the beginning:

1. Increased awareness of their racial misconceptions and stereotyped thinking as documented by pre- and posttests.
2. Quality of written and visual work (journals, drawings, etc.). I considered degrees of individual improvement.
3. Interaction with peers about social and artistic ideas and beliefs.

CONCLUSIONS

I conceived this program for inner-city high school students who face abuse in impoverished environments. Drugs, crime, and violence are part of their lives. The mural project challenged some of the students' beliefs: that human quality is racially determined, that one's own religion is superior to all others, that art is for the few, and that myths are silly stories. Tom Harper (1988) describes myths: "Discover the basic myth of any race, tribe, or culture, and you have the keys to their values, goals, and sense of meaning. Smash those myths while putting nothing in their place and humans become alienated, zapped of vigor and creativity" (p. A20).

The Cultural Myth-Centered Art Curriculum helped students to see the differences between "insider" and "outsider" knowledge (Headland, Pike, & Harris, 1990)—that is, the dual disparities between how they initially perceived other groups and how members of other groups perceived them. Finally, the program taught the students that their voices are valued by others, including authority figures from whom they were once estranged. My conclusion is that art-based, socially aware pedagogies can give students opportunities to explore the cultural traditions of others as they affirm their own.

NOTES

[1]The principal and the coordinator of the student program at SPHS Annex and the principal of SPHS assisted in this program. Funding came from NYU's School of Education, the New York School Board, and the SPHS Alumni Association.

[2]Elements that fostered intergroup harmony in this project include increasing participants' familiarity with other racial groups, creating a feeling of safety for participants' discussions about race, and enthusiastic participation by authority figures.

REFERENCES

Barfield, S. (1995). *Ethnic conflict in schools.* New Jersey: Enslow.

Devine, J. (1996). *Maximum security: The culture of violence in inner-city schools.* Chicago: University of Chicago Press.

Harper, T. (1988). Old myths are important to society. *Globe and Mail* (Toronto), 10 April, p. A20.

Headland, N., Pike, K., & Harris, M., eds. (1990). *Emics and etics: The insider/outsider debate.* California: Sage.

Remier, B., & Smith, R., eds. (1992). *Arts education and aesthetic knowing. 1991 yearbook of the National Society for the Study of Education.* Chicago: University of Chicago Press.

Walker, D. (1995). *Violence in schools: How to build a prevention program from the ground up,* Vol. 38, No. 5. Oregon School Study Council.

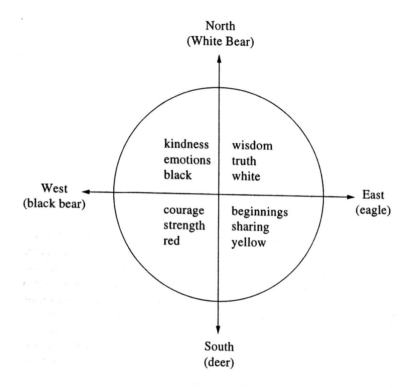

North
(White Bear)

kindness   wisdom
emotions   truth
black   white

West   East
(black bear)   (eagle)

courage   beginnings
strength   sharing
red   yellow

South
(deer)

**The Ojibwe Medicine Wheel
Kchitwa Kinoomaadwinaan**

CHAPTER 12

Simply Sacred

FUTURE AKINS

The sacred within my life is not a passing thought or a once-a-week ritual, but a moment-by-moment awareness, an awareness that is one of the most powerful sources feeding my hunger for art. Yet seeking what is sacred to each of us was never mentioned in my art classes. At times, I had discussed with friends, teachers, and students the sacred arts of faraway cultures and ancient religions, but we never talked about the sacred as a source of creative power, about what it meant to each of us. I did not realize that the sacred could be mine in my art and in my teaching. In fact, my art teacher preparation courses and studio classes had subtly warned me from expressing or exploring any form of the sacred.

In the summer of 1997, at the Spirituality in Education symposium at the Naropa Institute in Boulder, Colorado, I began to understand how creativity is linked to the sacred within each of us. Writer and educator Parker Palmer spoke of humanity's need to return to the sacred. Quietly, in his gentle manner, he defined the sacred as that which we hold with respect. Suddenly I understood: *that* was the essence of my work. That which I hold with respect is the sacred and is the source of my creativity. In turn, I seek the sacred within my art, through my art, and as my art. It is within me and at the same time beyond me.

In this paper I describe how I enact in the classroom a process for seeking one's sacred ideals and sharing them with others. I describe how I use the sacred as a guide. The process is complex and difficult, yet clear. It involves continuously respecting oneself, one's surroundings, and others in our every word and action both inside and outside the art classroom.

RESPECTING SELF

First I nourish the sacred within myself. If I don't take care of myself, I have nothing left to share with anyone. I become an empty voice repeating words without commitment, words that have no meaning or passion. How one takes care of oneself may vary, but I place aside time for silence and meditation every day. I practice the poetic movement of Tai Chi. I take long walks. I watch slow sunsets. What is important is that I still my inner noise.

Most significantly, I nourish the sacred within me through art. I allow myself time to be frustrated with a piece when it is not working. Time to get lost within a piece when it is working. Time to feel the thrill of finishing a piece, especially one I had thought impossible. Without this involvement with the creative process, I lose my ability to encourage and appreciate the journeys of my students.

RESPECTING PLACE

I honor the physical place where I am, whether my classroom, studio, or a hallway. I am grateful for the opportunities, and I delight in the possibilities. I do not ignore improvements that can be made, but I accept the present.

A part of honoring my surroundings is respecting equipment and supplies. Of course I want the best of both, but I have found that an art room filled with expensive equipment and supplies and students who lack self-worth or respect for their surroundings is an art room in a superficial sense. An art room with almost no equipment or supplies, however, filled with confident students with a sense of adventure, can be a thriving art community. I have witnessed beautiful creations drawn in pencil on notebook paper and even on paper plates by students energized to share their visual ideas with others.

I encourage the creative force in other ways, too. I include music and food when possible—music because it is a form of creative energy and food because sharing is essential to discovery. The music usually begins with pieces from my eclectic collection, and then students share their favorite pieces. Our rule is fifteen minutes for each person's music. If I hear complaints about "that kind of music" or "their music," all students lose their privileges, and I select the music for the rest of the day. They learn that such complaints violate the most important rule in my class: respect for self, surroundings, and others. Food sharing, whether simple snacks or entire meals, forms community. It nourishes our spirits, generates conversation, and provides energy.

RESPECTING OTHERS

I acknowledge the sacred within others: students, teachers, administrators, and staff. I dismiss what I perceived as past failures or accomplishments and attend to the present moment. Our exchanges are alive with possibilities because the past does not interfere with my expectations. I remind myself that we all constantly change, grow, and adjust.

An art class I taught for youth in substance recovery through Texas Tech University's Saturday ARTery program taught me a new way to see the sacred within my students. I allowed them to generate the curriculum. I released my need to have control of my students' artistic pursuits. I trusted the flow of student creativity to lead the way. I found that curiosity and self-discovery are sufficient motivators. Inclusion of the personal allowed everyone to take part. Art should not be an assignment. Students should experience it as unpredictable, uncontrollable, and unexpected. They should experience triumph even when hard work and good intentions leave nothing tangible. Art is one of our most powerful means to make the sacred real.

An example of this letting go of my authority occurred during our lunch break one Saturday. As we enjoyed pizza and soft drinks, I asked the students what they wanted to do next.

"I don't know."

"Whatever."

"Anything."

"What do y'all do outside of school?"

"Three of us have a band."

Then the conversation caught fire.

"Where do you play?"

"What kind of music do you play?"

This led to comparisons with other bands and opinions about what makes "a great concert." "Let's do something for their band!" one young woman suggested. More discussion followed about creating T-shirts and posters. Then the young woman, who had been working out a design on her soiled paper plate, suggested that the group make a large painted backdrop for the band. Everyone grabbed paper plates and began sketching ideas for a backdrop, freely sharing ideas and bluntly critiquing one another's work.

This conversation led to a second idea: making a slide show of these drawings to flash against the backdrop, since a static mural could not convey the constant change that they all felt in their lives. Someone suggested choreographing a performance incorporating the slides and the backdrop, so the nonmusicians could take part.

Asking me for advice and ideas, the students created their art curriculum for the next three weeks. My role was participant rather than sole creator. If we allow students to pursue their ideas, we may teach more than our planned lessons can. We define art as a self-motivated process that expresses what is important to us. The evolving process of respect for others includes accepting students as teachers and listening fully. Both tasks are demanding but necessary.

Students as Teachers

One winter day in a class of twenty-seven seventh graders, many of whom had cognitive and behavioral problems, I offered students a "free day" to complete unfinished work or to explore new ideas. I noticed unusual quiet in one corner of the room, a corner normally noisy with the antics of three young men skilled in finding reasons not to do assignments.

"I can't do this, Miss."

"It's too hard, Miss."

"Can I go to the bathroom, Miss? Really, it's an emergency."

As I approached the area, they turned and stared at me with big eyes and wide smiles. They had used their Formica desktops as pallets for mixing tempera paints with their hands. I began a stern lecture on neatness and use of materials when they held up their paint-covered hands and exclaimed, "Look, Miss! See the color we found!"

As I looked at the rich, soft, reddish brown that these three young artists had discovered, I realized that they were teaching me.

"How did you make this color?"

Speaking at once, they joyfully shared their discovery with me. We talked about how colors change, how dull or bright colors can be made, and our attraction to color. I suggested that they put their new color on different colors of paper to discover how differing backgrounds would affect it. I left with a gentle reminder about cleanup. I, an authority on color theory with abstract wheels and neat dots on trays, took away the joy of learning about color.

By the end of the period, they had concluded the experiment, deciding that they liked the color best "by itself." And they had cleaned up their corner, leaving not a speckle of paint anywhere, including on themselves. More important, three young men left knowing they had made a beautiful color.

As for me, I knew I had learned the most about color theory.

Listening

I have learned to listen to what is said, rather than what I expect to hear. I learned this lesson from the same ARTery class that made the band backdrop.

One Saturday morning, as the students entered the room, they found muffins and juice and two long tables covered with piles of bright cloth, remnant trimmings (lace, feathers, sequins, buttons, and other found objects), and various threads. Instrumental music was playing. Everyone, adults and aides included, was asked to enjoy a muffin, walk around, and select materials they found interesting. We were going to make Dream Dolls—doll forms made of cloth that conceal tokens or messages about ourselves that we wish to keep secret.

As our lunch break approached, I suggested that the students find a stopping place and begin to clean up. I walked around the room viewing the Dream Dolls. Some students had made three or four, while others had not finished one.

One student had no doll at all, although all morning I had watched him working diligently, sewing small stitches around a wizardlike figure. I asked him where his piece was.

"I threw it away."

I immediately went to the trash and started digging for it, muttering about how good it was and that nothing deserved to be thrown away. I found it—a beautiful work created with more detail than I had remembered. As I repeated how extraordinary I thought his doll was, he looked up at me through his long bangs and said, "I know. I threw it away on purpose."

I had crossed a boundary. "I messed up, didn't I?"

"Yep," he answered. By now the entire class was watching us, so I asked him if he wanted to go outside and talk privately. He nodded. Away from the stares of his peers, I asked, "Did you mean what you said about throwing it away on purpose?"

"Yes."

"Then let's do a ceremony with the doll, some sort of performance out in the courtyard of the art building." We walked outside into rain. As I looked for shelter, I turned to him at one point and noticed that the doll was gone. All I could say was, "Why?"

Looking me straight in the eye, he said, "So many beautiful things in this world are lost, and no one notices. It is important to make something as beautiful as possible, then let go of it, and to remember." Everything I understood about the sacred squeezed into that moment. I would never know the depths of this young man's life, but I surely had been witness to his pain and thoughtful reflection.

We went inside. As we walked upstairs, the students and the supervising professor met us, talking excitedly about the possibility of a videotaped performance. The young man listened to their ideas, smiled, and said quietly, "That's great, but you'd have to burn the tape." This notion surprised and interested them even more as they began to realize the young man's commitment to leaving no trace of his expression. Students remarked that he was the poet among them. All respected his creative act.

I end each day with a giving of thanks. I start with a deep breath to release the day's judgments. I reflect on the day's events. I ponder the joy, the pain, the excited voices, and the watching eyes. This reflection often occurs as I organize supplies and gather my things to leave the classroom.

Sometimes this moment occurs when a lingering student has one more question or observation to share. A young woman in one of my Drawing I classes, who "had to" research some artworks for an out-of-class assignment reluctantly visited a local gallery.

She was surprised when the owner gave her several brochures about the gallery's artists and, when learning about her assignment, a tour of the storage area to view more works. The respect offered her by the gallery owner made her feel like part of the larger art world.

When a classmate, excited about his new tattoo, heard her story, he asked if he could complete the same assignment by researching the history of body art. "Yes," I replied.

He paused, and then asked, "Really?"

"Yes," I repeated.

He smiled and sighed with relief. He had learned that art includes what he holds sacred.

I felt grateful for my knowledge that art is a safe place for me, a place for hiding sometimes and other times for venturing out, a place to say things with images that I cannot with words. I knew it could also be a safe place for my students.

When we begin nourishing the sacred within ourselves, honoring the sacred around us, acknowledging the sacred in others, and being grateful for our opportunities, we begin to understand the sacred as humans, as artists, and as teachers. And we will bring the sacred into our classrooms.

CHAPTER 13

Identity, Sexuality, and Power: Art and the Media

MARY WYRICK

Mass media images often influence students more strongly than traditional visual arts. Here I present four media artists as exemplars for guiding students in critical art viewing and making. Hannah Höch, Claude Cahun, Cady Noland, and Adrian Piper use the media to create politically charged artwork. I also present art lessons from real-world classrooms that use these artists' work to expose students to political issues.

ART, POWER, AND IDENTITY

Artists, teachers, and students can combine social and aesthetic issues with specific studio art assignments by responding to media themes that relate to their experiences. Colleen Kelley, an elementary teacher, artist, and graduate student at Buffalo State University, set up a stark contrast between two copies of a photograph of the familiar celebrity Madonna. Kelley appropriated two copies of a black-and-white image of the pop star. She embellished one copy of the image with cues that evoke female sexuality, such as a sultry look and a red ribbon. The other copy contains visual cues evocative of a good schoolgirl, such as a buttoned collar and a pink ribbon. Kelley demonstrated how two identical images can be altered to express contradictory ideas. She explores how power is wielded by the sexually empowered Madonna and yielded by the muted schoolgirl. Inspired by Adrian Piper, Kelley critiqued media stereotypes of women's sexuality.

ADRIAN PIPER: VANILLA NIGHTMARES
IN THE *NEW YORK TIMES*

Contemporary artist Adrian Piper alters newspaper pages by marking out, whiting out, and erasing directly onto them. With these markings, she critiques racism and sexism by revealing prejudices covertly present in the texts and images. In 1986, for example, she produced *Vanilla Nightmares 2, 3, 4, 9,* and *12* and *Poison,* a series of drawings on top of stories and advertisements from the *New York Times.* In *Vanilla Nightmares* she drew figures and faces of African Americans to cover, and seemingly invade, the newspaper. In *Vanilla Nightmares 4* Piper drew a muscular, nude, bald, black woman over an article about violence in Johannesburg, South Africa. The woman seductively looks at us over her shoulder. "But what if . . . ?" is handwritten over the text above an image of former South African president de Klerk, who, nude and on his hands and knees, fearfully looks up at us. On the floor is a noose placed near his head. Piper is asking, "What if . . . " this powerful white man were at the mercy of the black seductress?

Piper's newspaper art mingles politics, sexuality, violence, and racism. She alters these public accounts of news events into images of fantasy from a subconscious world. In *Vanilla Nightmares 3* and *12* and *Poison* Piper used *New York Times* advertisements to explore sexuality. In *3* and *Poison* she drew black men caressing an ad's white female model with huge hands. In *Poison* the men have blank white eyes and mouths. In *3,* an ad for Safari perfume, the man is snarling. Piper confronts the stereotype that black men are superhumanly endowed, uncontrollably sexual, and thus threatening to white women. She is also commenting on the poison of interracial taboos.

In *Vanilla Nightmare 12* a white-coated black couple drawn by Piper proffer to viewers a young model wearing a see-through dress. The Bloomingdale's ad reads "Say Yes," while a news story directly above reads "Around the World." The model's downcast, sulking, but sexy pose becomes mute, dispassionate acceptance in Piper's reconstruction. One is struck by how easily the original Bloomingdale's ad is altered to suggest a woman's sullen complicity in giving up her body. Piper's juxtapositions of images jolt us into recognizing our own positions of oppression or privilege.

Student teacher Laura King addressed how media constructions of women affect women's self-images. Based on the work of artist Barbara Kruger, King's work was made for a unit on representations of women.

This work appropriated an advertisement depicting an emaciated model with unnaturally long legs. Like Piper, King draws attention to how fashion iconography shapes women's and men's perceptions of women. King enjoins viewers to ignore imposed expectations and "Think for Yourself."

HISTORICAL PRECEDENTS IN VISUAL CRITIQUES OF POWER: HANNAH HÖCH

Dadaists believed artists had a social responsibility to address the upheavals in Europe in World Wars I and II. Dada artist Hannah Höch saw media words and images as opportunities to subvert a Germany headed toward Nazism. She challenged Western rationality by radically altering media images. Like other dadaists, she undermined the assumption of the Industrial Revolution that technological development means progress.

In *Cut with the Kitchen Knife* (1919), Höch photomontaged news photography and advertising images to parody and deconstruct European political power. Helmeted heads, officers stiffly posed in decorated uniforms, and austere faces of military leaders juxtapose with cogs and wheels that seem to trammel other figures. The oversized heads are often irreverently printed over with the word *Dada*. Grotesquely disproportional, mustached faces teeter on the diminutive bodies of ballerinas. Several decapitated ballerinas, faceless women, and crowds of anonymous heads signify pain, voicelessness, and dismemberment.

Höch used photographs from bourgeois news sources to criticize fascist leaders, subverting their power by contrasting their images with banal, humorous, and incongruent images. Höch's art is a form of nonviolent activism against oppression. Our students can use her methods of appropriation to express their own criticisms of issues such as militarism, media violence, or the benefits (or, as dadaists believed, the degradation) of new technologies.

CLAUDE CAHUN AND THE ART OF *CONTRE-ATTAQUE*

Surrealism, an art movement that existed formally in the 1920s and 1930s, explored dream images and the subconscious. Surrealists viewed repressed, primal insights as alternatives to rationality and logic. Lucy Schwob, a Jewish political activist and surrealist artist, worked in Nazi Germany and was forced to use the pseudonym Claude Cahun.

Cahun moved in 1937, together with her friend Suzanne Malherbe, from Paris to La Roquaise, on the British Channel island of Jersey. When the German army occupied Jersey in 1940, Cahun and Malherbe decided to stay and became active in the Resistance. On July 25, 1944, they were arrested by the Gestapo and condemned to death on November 16, 1944. On February 20, 1945, they were pardoned but kept in prison until May 1945, when the British army freed the island. Cahun stayed in Jersey until her death in 1954 (personal communication from K. Buol-Wischenau, Neue Galerie Graz, Munich, March 12, 1999).

Cahun felt that photography redefined perceptions of reality, and she used it to show that the "appropriateness" of one's societal role depends on cultural context. Surrealistic themes are popular among students today, and by studying artists such as Cahun, they can combine surrealistic inspiration with themes of power, oppression, and gender identity.

Like Höch, Cahun used photomontage to explore identity. She comments on subjective biases and androgyny in her portraits. In *Poupee I* (1936) Cahun photographed a standing figure constructed of newspaper. The doll has squared shoulders, an official-looking hat on a large masculine head, big feet, and crumpled flowers in its hands. The newspaper may have been simply an expedient sculpture medium, but its temporality and ability to evoke masculine authority come into play. If it is a doll, a potent surrealistic surrogate child, it is a hastily constructed product of cultural and material poverty. Doll or suitor, it can be trashed with today's newspaper. Teachers can use Cahun's works to discuss how identity, gender, class, and power are negotiated. Cahun's life and work show that definitions of "appropriateness" can change abruptly when political power changes hands. Conveying understanding of how power is encoded in objects and images is arguably a central mission of the art education field today.

CADY NOLAND: APOCALYPTIC POP-UPS

By studying the work of media and art theorists as well as contemporary artists such as Cady Noland, students can combine current events and contemporary art to explore cultural power and violence. Noland appropriates media images to comment on the celebrity status of violent criminals.

Noland's *Frame Device and Oozwald* relies on our collective memory of the live media killing of Lee Harvey Oswald, accused assassin of John F. Kennedy. A large printed aluminum pop-up figure of Oswald depicts his familiar doubled-over grimace at the moment of the shooting.

Oversized round holes punched into the figure symbolize bullet holes. His mouth is stuffed with a U.S. flag. The Oswald figure is part of an installation of beer cans pushed into piles against flimsy barricades—an American landscape clogged with trash and smelling of alcohol.

Noland's subjects are infamous celebrities placed within "abandoned" sites to be "discovered" by museum visitors. Noland borrows notorious media personae to evoke pervasive qualities of deviance in the trash-strewn landscapes of her installations.

Another Noland installation, *Tanya as a Bandit,* refers to heiress and kidnap victim Patty Hearst. Noland produced an aluminum pop-up of the famous beret-and-machine-gun image recorded by a bank video monitor. According to critic Meyer Rubinstein (1990), the Hearst figure, like the Oswald figure, is placed among detritus and miscellanea: "bungee cords, metal clips, flippers, snorkel, revolver, folded American flags, horse blankets, hamburger buns, potato chips, a vapor mask . . . and silkscreened sheets . . . of Patty Hearst and her family" (p. 160).

Noland's work would be especially appropriate for deconstructing the media attention accorded to young people who shoot their classmates and teachers. Instead of presenting violence as entertainment, she critiques the media magnification of violent personalities. In Noland's apocalyptic world, people use new technologies to escape in a society that is becoming unglued. Teachers can use her works as historical documents that question the increase in violent crimes by children.

YOUR CLASSROOM AS A SUBVERSIVE SITE

Your students can make art based on the critical approaches of these four artists by manipulating news photographs or texts for political ends. They can juxtapose images of weapons with societal refuse such as automotive and computer parts to create mechanical and cyber mixes of human and machine.

For example, Rick Scaduto, a student teacher at Buffalo State, combined a marker drawing with a newspaper story of the 1992–1993 invasion of Somalia. Because the initial battle occurred during the Christmas season, Scaduto's Santa wore insignias of the Soviet Union and the United States. Scaduto's Santa is a blind cyborg mix of tank, machine gun, and jolly benefactor.

George Gilham, another Buffalo State student teacher, responded to the invasion of Somalia by developing lessons about media images. He asked junior high school students to identify political issues in the media, find photographs representing their issues, render the photographs in charcoal, and add text to express their opinions.

Gilham produced his own poster as an example. He drew a chef's hat on a widely publicized photograph of a young prisoner of war. By ironically altering the photograph, he underscored the futility of U.S. efforts to be caregiver to the world and the morality of endangering U.S. soldiers in the process.

These artist/teachers created artwork and lessons that challenge media-fed cultural assumptions. Such challenges can help reverse social inequities. News and art are equally propagandistic, but what we will find in tomorrow's textbooks is the "truth" of today's news, not today's art. Art classes can provide nonviolent means to discover "truths" that conflict with media portrayals. Subversive art teachers offer ways for students to question what they "know."

REFERENCES

Rubinstein, M. R. (1990). Cady Noland. *Flash Art, 151,* 160.

CHAPTER 14

Sexual Identity in the Art Room

LAUREL LAMPELA

Today's prevailing art educational philosophies can be ranked according to their depth. Some emphasize the technical skills needed to make art, recommending that teachers focus on media, processes, elements, and principles (Herberholz & Herberholz, 1994; Wachowiak & Clements, 1997). Others include these factors but emphasize historical and critical inquiry (Eisner, 1987; Hurwitz & Day, 1995). Still others incorporate all of the above but stress the sociocultural contexts in which art is created (Cahan & Kocur, 1996; McFee & Degge, 1977).

In keeping with a growing trend across the general curriculum (Governor's Commission on Gay and Lesbian Youth, 1993; Jennings, 1992; Uribe & Harbeck, 1992), many art educators who teach from the third position include sexual identity in their curricula (Check, 1997; Honeychurch, 1995; Lampela, 1996). Acknowledging contributions of gays and lesbians in all content areas can positively affect both homosexual and heterosexual students (D'Augelli, 1992).

Gay and lesbian issues are becoming more visible in art education; however, teachers who are eager to include these issues may be uncertain how to do so. Countless art books discuss art by homosexual artists without discussing the artists' sexual identities, but no book until this one has addressed how to include sexual identity in public school art curricula. This chapter provides means for discussing artists' sexual identities in classrooms.

DOES DISCUSSING THE SEXUAL IDENTITY
OF ARTISTS MEAN TALKING ABOUT SEX?

Discussing lesbian and gay artists in art class does not mean discussing their sex lives[1] any more than discussing heterosexual artists means discussing theirs. In conversations about Georgia O'Keeffe teachers may want to mention her relationship with Alfred Stieglitz because his showing of her paintings was instrumental in her early success. Students are unlikely to think that mentioning O'Keeffe's marriage to Stieglitz must lead to discussing the couple's sexual behavior.

Art teachers may introduce sexual orientation for various reasons. One may be to aid in-depth study of a particular artist. In *Contemporary Art and Multicultural Education* Susan Cahan and Zoya Kocur (1996) suggest that teachers ask questions about work by David Wojnarowicz that explores the oppression of gays for simply being who they are (p. 299). The authors further suggest discussions on how homophobia equates to other forms of discrimination.

A second reason art teachers may introduce sexual identity is to answer students' art-related questions about gay or lesbian issues. Students may wonder why mention of heterosexual artists' personal relationships is commonplace while those of homosexual artists are ignored.[2] When the work of Sonia or Robert Delaunay, Frida Kahlo or Diego Rivera, Lee Krasner or Jackson Pollock, or Elizabeth or Willem De Kooning is discussed, their heterosexuality is made visible by mere mention of their marriages. However, despite the influence of Robert Rauschenberg's relationship with Jasper Johns in the meanings of certain of Rauschenberg's works (Katz, 1993), little or no reference is likely to be made to it.

A third reason teachers might raise lesbian and gay issues in class is to support students who are lesbian or gay or children of lesbian or gay parents. Part of good teaching is making one's classroom a safe zone for them. Teachers can mark safe zones in several ways. One is to post rainbow stickers in classrooms or hallways. Another is to display Safe Zone signs on windows, doors, and bulletin boards. The signs may take the form of a pink triangle with the letter Z in rainbow colors over it. The words *ally, safe zone,* or *safety zone* may be printed on the signs. The signs convey that the designated space is free from harassment, discrimination, and degrading jokes and language. Teachers also can display posters highlighting the contributions of gay and lesbian artists.

WHY ARE ARTISTS' SEXUAL IDENTITIES IMPORTANT?

In a 1996 presentation at the Ohio Art Education Association conference, I demonstrated why acknowledging an artist's sexual identity can be important. Participants completed a questionnaire about Marsden Hartley's *Indian Fantasy* and *Portrait of a German Officer*. The questions asked what the participants saw, what they thought the work meant, and their degree of ease in providing interpretations.

Most agreed that the theme of *Indian Fantasy* is Native American spirituality. This interpretation coincides with Joseph Covington's (1988). Many had greater difficulty interpreting *Portrait of a German Officer*, although they had much to say about the formal elements. I then mentioned Hartley's gayness and the fact that he loved Karl von Freyburg, a World War I German officer who was killed in battle. Participants found this extrinsic information valuable in understanding the painting. They then reinterpreted several of its formal elements as coded symbols.

Hartley completed at least twelve paintings in his *War Motif* series (McDonnell, 1995). Providing viewers with the circumstances of Hartley's life is essential to understanding the series. On the other hand, discussing his sexual behavior would be as unprofessional as discussing a heterosexual artist's sexual behavior. My experience with the Ohio audience demonstrates how omitting an artist's sexual identity can amount to depriving students of a complete education.

WHAT DOES ART-WORLD LESBOPHOBIA LOOK LIKE?

Teachers frequently teach the work of homosexual artists, often unaware of the artists' sexual orientation. The gayness of male artists—Michelangelo, Caravaggio, Charles Demuth, David Hockney, Robert Indiana, Andy Warhol, Robert Mapplethorpe, and Keith Haring—is better known than the lesbianism of female artists.

The lesbianism of female artists is less well known for a number of reasons. Women artists in general have received less attention than male artists (Collins & Sandell, 1984). During the 1970s art history texts such as H. W. Janson's (1971) *History of Art* and Helen Gardner's (1986) *Art Through the Ages* contained no references to women artists. Current editions include small numbers of women artists without reference to their sexual identities (Ashburn, 1996).

Until recently, information about lesbian artists was scattered. Only in recent years have we seen publications focused exclusively on lesbian artists, and nearly all have been published outside the United States.[3] The opposite is true for gay male artists.[4]

Despite the diversity of work by lesbian artists, one subgenre has received sensationalistic attention—the explicitly sexual imagery of artists such as Nicole Eisenman, Jo Darbyshire, and Della Grace. Using such work in a middle school or high school curriculum would be as unwise as using work that depicts heterosexual activities.

A CONTEXTUAL APPROACH TO UNDERSTANDING WORK BY A LESBIAN ARTIST

Lesbian British artist Sadie Lee does not focus on sexual activity.[5] Lee depicts lesbians in *Raging Bull, La Butch en Chemise,* and *Erect. Erect* depicts Lee seated next to her partner. When asked on an application form what her relationship was to the figures represented, Lee wrote, "Self-portrait with partner" (Horne & Lewis, 1996).

As with much work by lesbian and gay artists, Lee's work requires background. Cherry Smyth (1996) characterizes Lee as a painter of camp portraits and parodies of old masters. *La Butch en Chemise* lampoons Picasso's *La Femme en Chemise* by replacing the innocent female with a streetwise dyke who confronts the viewer with a penetrating stare.

Femme means woman in French, and in colloquial English it means feminine lesbian. Lee painted the opposite of a femme—a butch. Students might consider the uses of the words *femme* and *butch* in other languages and their meanings in historical and contemporary America. Have their meanings changed over time? How is reference to a woman as butch or a man as femme perceived in the heterosexual community?

Similarities and differences between the two paintings can spark discussion. In each the mood is somber as the solitary figure stands against a dark background. But how differently do the figures' clothing and stances affect viewers? In Picasso's portrait the figure wears a loose-fitting, sleeveless garment. She appears vulnerable, even timid. Her left nipple is noticeable beneath her transparent garment. In contrast, Lee's figure wears a denim vest and baggy jeans, and no emphasis is placed on her breasts. Can one's clothing assert one's sexual identity? Lee intended to portray a woman who is obviously lesbian. Does she accomplish this? Can the sexual identity of the Picasso female be ascertained? Students may assume that the intended viewers of much Western art are heterosexual males, but Lee's work points out that women, gay men, and lesbians view art too. What do the positions of the figures' heads convey? The head posture of Lee's figure conveys confidence. In contrast, the head of Picasso's figure is turned away from the viewer. Lee (1996) discusses this difference: "In a traditional painting of a female nude by a male artist, the woman in the painting is arranged in such a position as to appear available, unthreatening and entirely submissive to the male artist and viewer. She . . . looks away, while her body language still invites the viewer's attention" (p. 122).

Students could study figurative works by Caravaggio, Michelangelo, Donatello, Hosmer, Lewis, and others to determine if their choices of stance or clothing communicate the sexual identities of the figures or the artists themselves. Through their own art production, students could focus on how manipulating a figure's clothing, stance, or hair can express sexual identity.

LOOKING LESBIAN IN THE ART
OF ROMAINE BROOKS

Clothing and hair indicate sexual identity in the art of Romaine Brooks (1874–1971). Her lover Natalie Barney wrote revised lesbian history and poetry in the tradition of Sappho and held literary salons in her Parisian home. Brooks painted several of the salons' patrons. Accurate reading of these works requires discussing sexual identity. Brooks painted most of these women as identifiably lesbian, as she did herself at age 49 in *Self-Portrait* (1923). She wears a black top hat, black jacket, and gloves. Another portrait is of Una, Lady Troubridge, who was involved with Radclyffe Hall, author of *The Well of Loneliness*, a novel about lesbian life. Troubridge displays recognizable signs of the lesbian culture of 1920s Paris: a short haircut, a tailored shirt, a suit jacket, a monocle, and earrings (Garber, 1992). In a third portrait, Brooks depicts Renata Borgati as a handsome, short-haired musician in a black cape, seated at a piano. One might mistake Borgati for a man. Brooks also completed a portrait of the artist Gluck titled *Peter, a Young English Girl*. Gluck is depicted smoking a pipe in distinctively lesbian attire: black coat, leather belt, and necktie.

In a portrait of Natalie Barney, Brooks departed from 1920s representations of lesbians. She portrayed Barney dressed in a fur shawl, a conventional women's garment of the time. She may have done this to appease Barney, who despised the image of the mannish lesbian presented by sexologists of the early twentieth century.

Students might first view these portraits without extrinsic information about Brooks. They might recognize that the females in four of the five portraits are dressed in men's clothing. They might explore the varied reasons that women would choose to disguise themselves as men prior to the mid-twentieth century, when cross-dressing became legal (Garber, 1992; Faderman, 1991).[6]

Students could also measure changes in attitudes about cross-dressing by critiquing images of entertainers such as k. d. lang, Annie Lennox, Madonna, and the androgynous models in advertisements of the 1990s. A studio project might involve students' explorations into how identities are expressed through clothing and body ornamentation and how the media participate.

SEXUAL IDENTITY AS MUSE

Gluck was an out lesbian artist who expressed her sexual identity through her work. Her relationships with women influenced her paintings more than did aesthetic theories (Souhami, 1988). During a relationship with Constance Spry, a florist, she painted *The Vernon Picture,* a flower painting commissioned by one of Spry's clients, Lord Vernon (Souhami, 1988). Gluck completed at least two paintings of herself with Nesta Obermer, the woman she remained with until she died. In one, Gluck and Obermer are depicted romantically lazing in their boat.

Students could begin their investigation of this work by describing what they see. The sexual identities of the figures are difficult to discern. Some may describe them as a romantic couple, assuming that they are heterosexual. They might compare this work to paintings of similar subjects by Cassatt, Renoir, and others. What feelings do such works evoke? Teachers could then provide students with information about Gluck and Obermer and ask if this information changed how they view her painting. Does the image remain romantic? Why or why not? Was Gluck's vagueness in portraying the figures deliberate?

Medallion, a painting of Gluck with Obermer, celebrates their "marriage" in 1936. Gluck referred to it as the YouWe picture. After showing this work, teachers could show other works depicting artists with their sexual partners, such as Sadie Lee's *Erect,* Tee Corrine's *Self-Portrait with Lover and Camera,* David Hockney's *We Two Boys Together Clinging,* and Frida Kahlo's *Frida and Diego.* Each of these artists is lesbian, gay, or bisexual. Class discussion could address why parallel examples by heterosexual artists are so few. Lenore Chinn (1992), a lesbian artist, notes, "Making ourselves visible on our own terms becomes an important tool for self-empowerment. We need to identify who we are, document our lives and give shape to our visibility" (p. 21).

I once presented slides of work by Gluck and other lesbian artists to a group of lesbian art educators. They were proud of the strength of the work and angry that they had not seen it before. The artists became role models to these women, as lesbian and gay artists could become to our lesbian and gay students. They would learn that they are not alone, that others like them contribute to our art heritage.

EASIER THAN YOU THINK

Sexual identity is often irrelevant to artists' work, but at times it must be pointed out in the name of honest discussion. Yet misconceptions about what discussing sexual identity means may cause teachers to avoid it. Some contemporary lesbian and gay artists do erotic work, but an abundance of other gay and lesbian work addresses homosexual content without focusing on sexual activity. This work can be included in art curricula unless school districts expressly ban any mention of homosexuality. Few do.

Writing a chapter about including lesbian and gay content in class is one thing; implementation is another. Homosexuality can provoke emotional responses. Some students may deeply appreciate teachers who lead candid discussions about these issues. Others may express prejudices supported by their churches, parents, or other family members.

Teachers who approach a class with a relaxed attitude can steer discussions to a place of understanding. Referring to gender identity—gay or straight—when needed in order to understand art may teach students that everyone deserves dignity. Teacher implementation is a powerful means of change in schools. Excellent art teaching includes gay and lesbian artists' contributions and their sexual identities when appropriate. Excellent art teaching includes the contributions of all people.

NOTES

[1]In a letter to the editor of Art Education (1996, *49* (5), 5) the writer complained that the journal published an article that focused on the sex lives of artists. The article made no references to the sexual behavior of the artists but merely referred to the sexual identity of some artists.

²The relationships and marriages of heterosexual female artists are frequently mentioned in art books. See Chadwick, 1990; Heller, 1987; and Sutherland-Harris & Nochlin, 1976.

³Books devoted to the art by lesbian artists include Ashburn, 1996; Kelley, 1992; Smyth, 1996.

⁴See Blinderman, 1990; Celant, 1992; Gruen, 1991; Hockney, 1976; McDonnell, 1995; Valentine, 1994; Webb, 1989; and Wojnarowicz, 1992.

⁵Work by Sadie Lee has been included in Ashburn, 1996; Cooper, 1994; Horne & Lewis, 1996; and Smyth, 1996.

⁶Information about passing women can be found in Duberman, Vicinus, & Chauncey, 1989; and Faderman, 1991.

REFERENCES

Ashburn, E. (1996). *Lesbian art: An encounter with power.* Roseville East, Australia: Craftsman House.

Blinderman, B. (1990). *David Wojnarowicz: Tongues of flame.* Normal: University Galleries of Illinois State University.

Cahan, S., & Kocur, Z. (1996). *Contemporary art and multicultural education.* New York: Routledge.

Celant, G. (1992). *Keith Haring.* New York: Prestel.

Chadwick, W. (1990). *Women, art, and society.* London: Thames and Hudson.

Check, E. (1997). Queers in the classroom: Internalized and projected homophobia. In E. Check, G. Deniston, & D. Desai, Living the discourse. *Journal of Social Theory in Art Education, 17,* 56–70. Reston, VA: National Art Education Association.

Chinn, L. (1992). Visibility, identity, community. In C. Kelley, ed. *Forbidden subjects: Self-portraits by lesbian artists.* North Vancouver, British Columbia: Gallerie Productions.

Collins, G., & Sandell, R. (1984). *Women, art, and education.* Reston, VA: National Art Education Association.

Cooper, E. (1994). *The sexual perspective: Homosexuality and art in the last 100 years in the West.* London: Routledge & Kegan Paul.

Covington, J. (1988). Marsden Hartley: Indian fantasy. *Art Education, 41* (4), 37.

D'Augelli, A. R. (1992). Teaching lesbian/gay development: From oppression to exceptionality. In K. M. Harbeck, ed., *Coming out of the classroom closet: Gay and lesbian students, teachers, and curricula.* New York: Harrington Park.

Duberman, M., Vicinus, M., & Chauncey, G., Jr., eds. (1989). *Hidden from history: Reclaiming the gay and lesbian past.* New York: Meridan.

Eisner, E. (1987). *The role of discipline-based art education in America's schools.* Los Angeles: Getty Center for Education in the Arts.

Faderman, L. (1991). *Odd girls and twilight lovers: A history of lesbian life in twentieth-century America.* New York: Columbia University Press.

Garber, M. (1992). *Vested interests: Cross-dressing and cultural anxiety.* New York: Routledge.

Gardner, H. (1986). *Art through the ages.* San Diego: Harcourt, Brace, Jovanovich.

Governor's Commission on Gay and Lesbian Youth. (1993). *Making schools safe for gay and lesbian youth: Breaking the silence in schools and families* (education report). Boston: State House.

Gruen, J. (1991). *Keith Haring: The authorized biography.* New York: Prentice Hall.

Heller, N. G. (1987). *Women artists: An illustrated history.* New York: Abbeville.

Herberholz, D., & Herberholz, B. (1994). *Artworks for elementary teachers: Developing artistic and perceptual awareness.* Madison, WI: Brown & Benchmark.

Hockney, D. (1976). *David Hockney: My early years.* New York: H. N. Abrams.

Honeychurch, K. G. (1995). Extending the dialogue of diversity: Sexual subjectivities and education in the visual arts. *Studies in Art Education, 36* (4), 210–217.

Horne, P., & Lewis, R., eds. (1996). *Outlooks: Lesbian and gay sexualities and visual cultures.* London: Routledge.

Hurwitz, A., & Day, M. (1995). *Children and their art: Methods for the elementary school* (6th ed.). Fort Worth, TX: Harcourt, Brace, Jovanovich.

Janson, H. W. (1971). *History of art.* New York: Harry N. Abrams.

Jennings, K. (1992). Talking about lesbians/gays in regular high school history: Journal reflections. *Empathy, 3* (1), 29–31.

Katz, J. (1993). The art of code: Jasper Johns and Robert Rauschenberg. In W. Chadwick & I. de Courtivron, eds., *Significant others: Creativity and intimate partnership.* London: Thames and Hudson.

Kelley, C., ed. (1992). *Forbidden subjects: Self-portraits by lesbian artists.* (Gallerie, Women Artists' Monographs, No. 10)

Lampela, L. (1996). Gay and lesbian artists: Toward curricular inclusiveness. *Taboo: A Journal of Culture and Education, 2* (fall), 49–64.

Lee, S. (1996). Lesbian artist? In P. Horne & R. Lewis, eds., *Outlooks: Lesbian and gay sexualities and visual cultures.* London: Routledge.

McDonnell, P. (1995). *Dictated by life: Marsden Hartley and Robert Indiana.* Minneapolis: Frederick R. Weisman Museum, University of Minnesota.

McFee, J. K., & Degge, R. (1977). *Art, culture, and environment: A catalyst for teaching.* Dubuque, IA: Kendall/Hunt.

Smyth, C. (1996). *Damn fine art by new lesbian artists.* London: Cassell.

Souhami, D. (1988). *Gluck: Her biography.* London: Pandora.

Sutherland-Harris, A., & Nochlin, L. (1976). *Women artists 1550–1950.* New York: Random House.

Uribe, V., & Harbeck, K. M. (1992). Addressing the needs of lesbian, gay, and bisexual youth: The origins of PROJECT 10 and school-based intervention. In K. M. Harbeck, ed., *Coming out of the classroom closet: Gay and lesbian students, teachers and curricula* (pp. 9–28). Binghamton, NY: Harrington Park.

Valentine, F. (1994). *Tom of Finland: His life and times.* New York: St. Martin's.

Wachowiak, F., & Clements, R. D. (1997). *Emphasis art: A qualitative art program for elementary and middle schools* (6th ed.). New York: Longman.

Webb, P. (1989). *Portrait of David Hockney.* New York: Penguin.

Wojnarowicz, D. (1992). *Memories that smell like gasoline.* New York: Artspace Books.

PART IV

Real-World Structural Change: Rewriting the Rules

KAREN KEIFER-BOYD

The authors in Part IV present their experiences as facilitators of radical changes in school policy, curriculum, and teaching. This section informs us how to use guerrilla tactics to subvert sacred art educational doctrines, to relinquish teacher control of our students, to create self-sculptures on the Internet, and to replace power and control with transformative and participatory practices.

Part IV advocates participatory democracy by underscoring the need for aesthetic-expressive discourse. *Aesthetic-expressive discourse* refers to making decisions about sensory stimuli that influence us. Jürgen Habermas (1983) suggests that when a society ignores aesthetic-expressive discourse and emphasizes only moral, practical, and cognitive knowledge, the result will be rigorous doctrines devoid of human empathy. The interaction of cognitive approaches with moral-practical and aesthetic-expressive approaches "encourages social action and moral consciousness" (Blandy, 1987, p. 48). The chapters in Part IV offer advice on how to teach democratic participation in aesthetic-expressive discourse.

In Chapter 15, "A Field Guide for Art Educators: Guerrilla Tactics for Change," Gayle Marie Weitz and Marianne Stevens Suggs present a burlesque field guide of guerrilla tactics for art educators to resist those who protect universal notions. Weitz and Suggs describe a course of action in art education that includes aesthetic, emotional, and physical needs of the whole world's population, including plant and animal species. The authors identify six battles that art educators face if they intend to teach from a multicultural, social reconstructionist perspective.

123

Their guerrilla tactics mock unquestioned practices and provide radical solutions for life-affirming social change.

In Chapter 16, "Caught Between Control and Creativity: Boredom Strikes the Art Room," Ed Check critiques our culturewide reverence for domination and control in the classroom. He describes how he relinquished his power, and in so doing, empowered his sixth graders to take responsibility for their educations. This chapter concerns classroom structural changes in a K–12 setting as the author shares his experience negotiating social control and student power in the classroom. The author argues that the field of art perversely restructures the subject of art into an extremely dull and thereby dangerous methodology, a methodology primarily about form and not content. He also introduces a higher-education model for promoting radical change in preservice programs. The model's goal is to reveal ways of teaching other than those based in teacher control.

In Chapter 17, "Going Nowhere: Exploring the Cyberspace Between Our Ears," Michael J. Emme portrays education shifts from linear-text to nonlinear Internet sites and their hybrid forms of linked information. Emme visualizes the impact of the current transition of a linear, text-based society to nonlinear, electronic societies as children grow up with hypermedia. He challenges modernist assumptions of distinct disciplinarity. Hypermedia blur discipline boundaries as Internet users cross-link ideas according to their own explorative paths. Emme constructs a usable interdisciplinary, three-dimensional visual curriculum.

Karen Keifer-Boyd concludes Part IV with "By the People: A Community-Based Art Curriculum." She presents strategies she used to engage a rural community in developing an art curriculum based on local aesthetics. These consensus-building strategies involved participation by teachers, students, school administrators, and community members. Ten years after the district implemented the art program, she interviewed several original participants as well as new teachers to the school district to find out how the curriculum had evolved. She identifies factors that contributed to the project's initial success as well as to its maintenance.

Real-World Readings in Art Education provides art educational examples of participatory democracy, challenging theories, cutting-edge content, and critical methodologies. We are empowered when we question existing circumstances and include all perspectives in finding just and caring solutions.

REFERENCES

Blandy, D. (1987). Art, social action, and the preparation of democratic citizens. In D. Blandy & K. G. Congdon, eds., *Art in a democracy* (pp. 47–57). New York: Teachers College Press.

Habermas, J. (1983). Modernity: An incomplete project. S. Ben-Habid, trans. In H. Foster, ed., *The anti-aesthetic: Essays on postmodern culture* (pp. 3–15). Port Townsend, WA: Bay Press.

CHAPTER 15

A Field Guide for Art Educators: Guerrilla Tactics for Change

GAYLE MARIE WEITZ AND
MARIANNE STEVENS SUGGS

We live in a postmodern world, characterized by increasing amounts of change. Never before has so much changed, so fast, and with such dramatic implications (Connor, 1992). Can we art educators prepare our students and ourselves to deal with the twenty-first century?

ART: AN APPROPRIATE PLACE FOR EDUCATIONAL REFORM

We need to understand, appreciate, and tolerate those different from ourselves, question and compromise our materialistic and consumptive American lifestyle, and examine our relationship to the planet and its nonhuman inhabitants. With societal structures in disarray, the public turns to education to meet such needs in the twenty-first century. Where better than art to address these issues? Owing to its peripheral status, art is subject to few curricular prescriptions or standardized tests. Less encumbered than other subjects, it more easily accommodates new content such as broadened definitions of art created by the inclusion of marginalized peoples.[1] These broader definitions create multiple truths. Furthermore, art study involves multiple ways of knowing, including but not limited to the rational. Such comprehensive educational experiences are rare in schools and are becoming increasingly valued as we discover more about intelligence and differences between people (Gardner, 1993). Art education can be an effective, if not the best, vehicle for change. So, how can we conduct relevant postmodern art education in K–12 classrooms? Militant action is required!

GUERRILLA TACTICS FOR ART EDUCATORS

Art education witnesses skirmishes from time to time, but now we need serious action. What obstacles thwart needed shifts in art education? We have identified six decisive battles and corresponding guerrilla tactics for waging a postmodern "war" that must be won. Time is of the essence. Prepare for battle! Overcome the enemy! Guerrilla art warfare is now required!

Battle One: The Tyranny of the Formalist/Modernist Orientation

Most art teacher training[2] still consists of studio courses with modernist orientations.[3] These orientations are too narrow to account for contemporary definitions of art.[4] Often students encounter postmodern orientations only in their art education methods classes. Can such limited exposure offset the influence of those modernist studio classes?

Guerrilla Tactic One

Lobotomize the parts of modernist professors' brains that teach perspective, color wheels, and compositional techniques. Then hire the ad agencies that so successfully promoted smoking to kids. Their task is to implement a campaign ending the notion that "the best art teachers come from the pool of the best modernist, Western, fine artists."

Battle Two: The Despotic Rule of Western Art History

Art history classes constitute the remaining component of most art teachers' training. In these courses students learn primarily about the art of dead white Western European males (DWWEMs).[5] This bias is but a component of a larger set of discriminatory practices in our society (cf. Becker, 1994). Many art history departments recognize this and include courses in African or Asian art. But do art education majors have time to take such classes? Where do they acquire the knowledge to cope with issues of diversity?

Guerrilla Tactic Two

Instigate an affirmative action program for art history slide holdings, requiring that they reflect global demographics (51 percent women, 75 percent people of color, etc.) and that they be cataloged not only by country/media/artist but also by theme/content/message. Then put these images into public domain on the Internet.

Battle Three: The Outdated Practice of Many Art Educators, Compounded by Insufficient Opportunity for Retraining

Most art education training programs emphasize modernist studio orientations and white male art history. Therefore, most K–12 art programs emphasize this content, since many teachers teach what they were taught (Apple, 1979). How can we inspire art educators to update their views? Retraining is the traditional method, but few teachers today have time. So where do we find a catalyst for change?

Guerrilla Tactic Three

Teachers who attend art education conferences usually participate in media process and technique workshops. We advocate no longer granting renewal credits for such activities; instead, teachers will receive credit only for sessions on matters of societal and global concern. In addition, we call for supplying teachers with memberships to socially minded organizations such as the National Art Education Association's Caucus on Social Theory and Women's Caucus, Educators for Social Responsibility, and Teaching Tolerance.[6]

Battle Four: Inadequate Art Education Licensure and Curriculum Guidelines

State departments of public instruction perpetuate status quo notions of art through two entities: licensure and curriculum. The art licensure tests usually require only knowledge of modernist studio traditions and Western art history.[7] State art curriculum guides often reflect this bias.[8] Even if state licensures and curricula did include postmodern content, change would be slow because we don't have art ed police who can be called to scenes of heartbreak and tragedy caused by passé art education.

Guerrilla Tactic Four

Replace art certification "exit" tests with art educator detectors (AEDs), which look similar to airport metal detectors. Successful passage through an AED requires strong belief in the importance of art to life and all ramifications thereof. Unqualified candidates set off an alarm, signaling a need for intense postmodern art remediation or, failing that, alternative career counseling. Training for art ed police would be similar to that of Navy SEALs.

Battle Five: Debilitated Administrators and Public Officials

In public schooling those charged with hiring teachers and assessing what is taught in the art room are often administrators who consider the arts "extras" in education. They too often believe art cannot change or reflect societal conditions. Political officials seem to have even less knowledge of art.[9] With such crippling notions of art held by such powerful folks, art education remains stagnant or, worse, continues to slip into the abyss.

Guerrilla Tactic Five

Kidnap all administrators and elected officials and submit them to intensive training in which they learn to value visual culture. Then return them to their positions, secure in the knowledge that they will restructure the general curriculum. They will place art at the center, where it can integrate all other school subjects and be a catalyst for change. If the curriculum shows signs of relapsing toward a reading, 'riting, and 'rithmetic tradition, administrators will receive correction serums intravenously until symptoms cease. If symptoms persist, patients will be issued virtual reality helmets programmed to their biases. The patients can then perform their duties to virtual audiences only.

Battle Six: The Inappropriate Content of Advanced Placement Courses and College Entrance Portfolios

Many students consider advanced placement (AP) courses to be pinnacles of their art educations, and college entrance portfolio reviews often determine their admission into university art programs.[10] Both of these "art ed boot camps" are based, again, in modernist studio and white male art history traditions and therefore must be annihilated. How can art educators *ever* teach postmodern art education and risk their students' failing AP or being denied university entrance? It is the old chicken-and-egg question: Do you change the AP course and then the portfolio requirement, or do you change the portfolio requirement and then the AP course?

Guerrilla Tactic Six

Revamp AP courses to require studio work that expresses compelling ideas. No longer accept slides for university entrance. Instead, require applicants to submit resumes documenting public service, political activism, and other socially and environmentally minded activities, evidence of critical reasoning, and substantial knowledge of persons unlike themselves.

JOKING ASIDE: THIS IS SERIOUS BUSINESS!

These are our radical guerrilla tactics for victory. Although joking may save our sanity, the situation is serious. How can postmodern changes occur in art education without winning these battles? Ellen Friedman et al. (1996) remind us that Rome wasn't built in a day. Our field's incomplete curricula and inadequate pedagogy were not either. Conservatives commonly advise patience, pointing out that educational reform is historically slow. But do we have the luxury of time? Isn't our postmodern era characterized by its ever increasing rate of change?

Postmodern urgency requires that we not wait for recalcitrant obstacles to disappear funeral by funeral. The responsibility for change then rests, first, on the shoulders of individuals—you and me; second, on departments and schools; and third, on communities. We must cause small changes, remembering that they lead to big changes.[11] As Margaret Mead reminds us, never doubt that a small group of thoughtful, committed citizens can change the world. Indeed, it's the only thing that ever has.

IT'S UP TO US . . .

Each of us controls how much we contribute to this postmodern art educational transformation. Pat answers, recipe books, or even guerrilla field guides may not be there to help us. The power to change does not lie in them; it lies in us.

M. C. Smith and the authors of this chapter (1997) adapted Peggy McIntosh's (1984) Evolution of Feminism curriculum to transform a modernist art education departmental curriculum at Appalachian State University into an inclusive, postmodern curriculum. The content shifted from studio based and male European to gender and racially balanced. The methodology shifted from authoritarian lecture format to collaborative and student centered. These phases occur as follows:

Phase I: The art curriculum is Otherless—that is, the content contains references only to Western male fine arts.

Phase II: The art curriculum is somewhat inclusive; others are included in the curriculum, but only if they are capable of fitting into the dominant perspective. An example might be the inclusion of the sculptor Richard Hunt or the painter Romare Bearden (both African Americans) in a discussion of professional artists in the United States. This approach, often called additive, does nothing to help students understand how the dominant culture and other cultures are interconnected and interrelated, except to imply that to be included one must be perceived as "mainstream."

Phase III: The art curriculum is more inclusive, but others are included and referred to as problems, viewed as victims, as deprived, and/or defective. An example of such a titillating and shocking inclusion might be Frida Kahlo, who is often viewed as an "emotional woman" who was "self-taught." This ethnocentric outlook takes into account multiple points of view but regards those of other cultures as incorrect, inferior, or even immoral.

Phase IV: The art curriculum includes others, but keeps them separate; others are relegated to separate chapters, separate units, separate courses. An example is *Gardner's Art Through the Ages* (Tansey & Kleiner, 1996), in which "Part III—The World Beyond Europe" is set aside for non-Western material. Another example would be separate courses in African art, Asian art, or women artists.

Phase V: The art curriculum has been transformed to include others. (This is difficult to imagine in a climate that generates comments such as "but the work just isn't as good" or "but more inclusive I can't be; I already don't have enough time to cover the important artists.") The approach best suited appears to be a thematic one. Graeme Chalmers (1996) suggests a study of cross-cultural examples of art through which the makers have become ascribers of meaning, ascribers of status, catalysts of social change, enhancers and decorators, interpreters, magicians, mythmakers, propagandists, recorders of history, sociotherapists, storytellers, and teachers. He states that "with some knowledge of the functions and roles of art across cultures and a willingness to learn about art with students, multicultural art education is not as daunting as it may first appear" (p. 36). Even so, change must be holistic and multilayered. At this stage many realize "that cultural pluralism is a reality and that reluctant, grudging, or tacit recognition by one culture of another must be replaced by genuine appreciation and proactive corrective action; that no racial, cultural, or national group is inherently superior to another; that no one group's art is basically superior to another's; and that equality of opportunity, in the art classroom and elsewhere, is a right that must be enjoyed by every student regardless of ethnic, cultural, or other differences" (Chalmers, 1996, p. 2).

Phase VI: We have added a sixth stage, which James Banks (1989) refers to as a decision-making, social-action approach. Here, art education becomes an agent for social reconstruction; students view art as an agent to expose and challenge oppression.

In changing our own curricula, we might first ask: Do we know enough about ourselves and art? Are we prepared to be lifelong learners? Inertia or fear may threaten our quests for knowledge, but stimulation, accomplishment, and professional authenticity are our rewards. Chalmers (1996) suggests a shift from asking what is art to asking the why of art. He states, "Rather than viewing teachers as transmitters of huge bodies of knowledge, we should see them as leaders and facilitators who are able to focus on the process and assist students in their investigation and understanding of commonalities in the functions and roles of art across cultures" (p. 38).

We must recognize that a battle lurks around each corner. Such is life. Such is art education. Not only do our challenges change, but our solutions need to as well. A good solution in 2000 may be a poor solution in 2010. Changes, uncertainties, and challenges can be a valuable part of our teaching. Our strength enables us not only to cope with them but also to value them. Our confidence sees us through each battle. Advance and retreat; advance and retreat. On to victory!

NOTES

[1]Works by Lucy Lippard (1990), Suzi Gablik (1995), and Susan Cahan and Zoya Kocur (1996), for example, contain marginalized voices in art educational contexts.

[2]See the *National Visual Arts Standards* of the National Art Education Association (NAEA), the requirements of the National Association of Schools of Art and Design (NASAD), the standards of the National Council for the Accreditation of Teacher Education, and the requirements of state departments of public instruction. One reason for studio dominance is the belief held by many "that primary and secondary art teachers who exhibit a high level of skill as artists and designers are generally more effective" (NASAD, 1995, p. 96).

[3]Postmodernists view art as an expression of culture, closely connected to and often critical of human affairs and social conditions. This view contrasts with the modernist view of art as preoccupation with originality, creativity, pure abstraction, disinterested perception, and aesthetic experience. Such a major shift within the art world suggests the rethinking of existing art educational paradigms.

[4]Graeme Chalmers (1996) discusses the ethics involved in defining art and how narrow definitions exclude people. Arthur Danto (1992) discusses the

changing notions of art and the ways in which artists work. Ellen Dissanayake (1988) discusses the definition of art in reference to the role it plays in life, that is, "making special" (p. 42).

[5]Examples of popular art history survey texts are Janson's *History of Art* (1991) and Tansey and Kleiner's *Gardner's Art Through the Ages* (1993). H. W. Janson's book mentions three thousand men artists but no women artists. The edition revised by A. F. Janson, son of H. W. Janson, mentions nineteen women artists.

[6]Teaching Tolerance can be reached at 400 Washington Ave., Montgomery, AL 36104. Educators for Social Responsibility can be reached at 23 Garden St., Cambridge, MA 02138, 1-800-370-2515.

[7]Most states require prospective teachers to pass national standardized tests (NTE, PRAXIS) to obtain teaching licenses. For example, questions from the PRAXIS art test are: "A photographer who wishes to show variations from high-lights to shadows would be most concerned with manipulation of which of the following elements? A. line, B. shape, C. value, D. texture, E. hue" and "The style and treatment of the figures of the sculpture shown above indicate that the work belongs to which of the following styles? A. Baroque, B. Superrealist, C. Romantic, D. Neoclassical, E. Renaissance" and "The process of producing a design by scratching through a layer of slip to expose the clay body underneath is called A. underglazing, B. slip trailing, C. stenciling, D. wax resist, E. sgraffito" (Educational Testing Service, 1996b, pp. 8–9). These sample questions are examples of the strong emphasis on the formalist orientation and the lack of inclusion of art and artists from non-Western traditions.

[8]State curriculum guides usually reflect standards set by the "experts" in the field. In art education this most often is the National Art Education Association (NAEA). The NAEA's *National Visual Arts Standards* consist of six general standards:

1. Understanding and applying media, techniques, and processes;
2. Using knowledge of structures and functions;
3. Choosing and evaluating a range of subject matter, symbols, and ideas;
4. Understanding the visual arts in relation to history and cultures;
5. Reflecting upon and assessing the characteristics and merits of their work and the work of others; and
6. Making connections between visual arts and other disciplines (1994, pp. 14–24).

All of these standards could be viewed from a status quo or a postmodern position. Such open-ended standards enable the dominance of the formalist/modernist/Western European orientation to continue, but they also open the door to postmodern change.

[9]A prominent example of such an official is North Carolina's senator Jesse Helms, who leads the way in distinguishing "good proper American art" from "bad art."

[10]In the AP handbook the portfolio requirements include sections addressing quality, concentration, and breadth. In order to meet the breadth requirements, each high school student must submit slides of eight works (either two- or three-dimensional) under the color/design category that must "demonstrate principles of visual organization, including color organization." The following example is given: "color organization using primary, secondary, tertiary, analogous, or other color subsets" (Educational Testing Service, 1996a, p. 10). And in the sculpture/three-dimensional design category, students are asked to submit four slides (at least two three-dimensional works), with the following example given: "formal work that embodies line, plane, mass, or volume" (Educational Testing Service, 1996a, p. 11).

The application process to most university-level art departments and professional art schools reveals a similar formalist bias. Acceptance into most art departments entails the submission of a slide portfolio of one's studio work. Application procedures usually include the criteria used for judging the slides. For example, the Art Department at Appalachian State University provides these criteria: "understanding of and sensitivity to the visual elements," "application of the principles of two-dimensional design and composition," and "application of the principles of three-dimensional design and composition" (Appalachian State University, 1996).

[11]Examples of small changes leading to bigger changes are: Ya/Ya, 628 Baronne St., New Orleans, LA 70113; K.O.S. (see Paley, 1995); SECCA's (Southeastern Center for Contemporary Art) Artist in the Community Program, 750 Marguerite Dr., Winston-Salem, NC 27106; and such community-oriented artists as Judy Baca (see Felshin, 1995).

REFERENCES

Appalachian State University. Art Department. (1996). *Foundations Portfolio Review Form*. Boone, NC: Author.

Apple, M. J. (1979). *Ideology and curriculum*. London: Routledge and Kegan Paul.

Banks, J. A. (1989). Integrating the curriculum with ethnic content: Approaches and guidelines. In J. A. Banks & C. A. McGee-Banks, eds., *Multicultural education issues and perspectives* (pp. 189–207). Boston: Allyn and Bacon.

Becker, C. (1994). *The subversive imagination: Artists, society, and social responsibility.* New York: Routledge.

Cahan, S., & Kocur, Z. (1996). *Contemporary art and multicultural education.* New York: New Museum of Contemporary Art.

Chalmers, G. (1996). *Cultural pluralism.* Los Angeles: Getty Institute for the Arts.

Connor, D. (1992). *Managing at the speed of change.* New York: Villard.

Danto, A. (1992). *Beyond the Brillo box.* New York: Farrar, Straus, Giroux.

Dissanayake, E. (1988). *What is art for?* Seattle: University of Washington Press.

Educational Testing Service. (1996a). *Advanced placement course description: Art.* Princeton, NJ: Author.

————. (1996b). *The PRAXIS series: Arts.* Princeton, NJ: Author.

Felshin, N. (1995). *But is it art? The spirit of art as activism.* Seattle, WA: Bay Press.

Friedman, E., Kolmar, W., Flint, C., & Rothenberg, P., eds. (1996). *Creating an inclusive college curriculum.* New York: Teachers College Press.

Gablik, S. (1995). *Conversations before the end of time.* London: Thames and Hudson.

Gardner, H. (1993). *Multiple intelligences: The theory in practice.* New York: Basic Books.

Janson, H. W. (1991). *History of art* (4th ed.). A. F. Janson, rev. New York: H. N. Abrams.

Lippard, L. (1990). *Mixed blessings.* New York: Pantheon.

McIntosh, P. (1984). The study of women: Processes of personal and curricular revision. *Forum for Liberal Education, 6* (5), 2–4.

National Art Education Association (NAEA). (1994). *The national visual arts standards.* Reston, VA: National Art Education Association.

National Association of Schools of Art and Design (NASAD). (1995). *National Association of Schools of Art and Design handbook.* Reston, VA: National Association of Schools of Art and Design.

Paley, N. (1995). *Finding art's place.* New York: Routledge.

Smith, M. C., Suggs, M. S., & Weitz, G. M. (1997). Efforts to diversify the art department curriculum. *Teaching and Learning at Appalachian, 1,* pp. 12–15. Boone, NC: Hubbard Center.

Tansey, R., & Kleiner, F. (1996). *Gardner's art through the ages.* New York: Harcourt Brace.

CHAPTER 16

Caught Between Control and Creativity: Boredom Strikes the Art Room

ED CHECK

Popular culture was where the action was—It marked out a territory where pleasure, knowledge, and desire circulated in close proximity to the life on the streets. . . . We felt rather than knew what was really useful knowledge. And we talked, danced, and lost ourselves in a street culture that never stopped moving. Then we went to school.

Something stopped us in school. For me, it was like being sent to a strange planet . . . what we learned had little to do with where we came from, who we were, or where, at least, we thought we were going.

HENRY GIROUX, 1994, PP. 6–7

EXAMINING RELATIONSHIPS BETWEEN CONTROL AND BOREDOM

Within the past year I have visited K–12 art classrooms in a variety of socioeconomic and racial contexts. As a university professor part of my task is to assess the performance of student teachers. Like many in art education, I value creativity, imagination, and critical thinking. Yet, my observations and conversations with students and teachers alike lead me to believe there is a serious paradox operating in art classrooms: creativity is compromised and control emphasized.

How do I know this? I know it because I am often bored in classes I attend and supervise: bored by the crayon and color-wheel banality of it all, listening to the same often picayune points being made over and over again. This boredom signifies to me a disturbing relationship between creativity and control. It suggests to me that excessive teacher control, student passivity, and content-restricted curricula create a classroom climate inhospitable not only to student inquiry but to self-expression itself. The field of art, inherently heroic and interesting, a field that produces rigorous social critique, is reduced to a glorified methodology in art education.

I observe teachers planning lifeless lessons that they pass off as art "activities." They spend inordinate amounts of time immobilizing students. Rarely do I witness students integrating their lived experiences into the classroom. "Real life" seems far too dangerous, chaotic, and controversial.

I have found that teachers are central to the patterns of this ennui. Why are certain teachers more creative or more controlling? Are students paying attention? Are they actively involved? Are they able to integrate the "stuff" of their lives? What relevant content do teachers allow into the curriculum? Do students see themselves as artists or as students? When teachers trust themselves and their students, they tend to get beyond their fear of "losing control" in the classroom. These classroom atmospheres differ significantly from tightly controlled ones. Students are openly curious, are more apt to share their ideas, have more humorous exchanges, and are eager to examine issues that touch their lives.

HOW I WAS TAUGHT TO TEACH

I learned that authority and control are necessities of school life (Wachowiak, 1977). Unintentionally, this set me up as "the expert." As expert, I had to know more than my students. In what Paulo Freire (1990) refers to as a banking model for teaching, I "filled" students with information. As a "responsible" teacher (1980–1989), I defined the curriculum, directed teaching, monitored student behavior, and assessed progress. Within such a teaching approach students depended on my interpretations and limited vision.

After three years of this I tired of controlling students' thoughts and moves. I also felt displeased with what I was offering students as art content. I began to question my methodology, one that I based primarily on the elements and principles of design. I realized school art activities were unrelated to the lives of my students. Consistency, routine, and a predictable plastic aesthetic had replaced inquiry and learning. Arthur Efland's (1976) notion of a school art style rang true. Students' art reflected school culture, not their lives. With little exception most art projects were similar in size, materials, and content. I unknowingly promoted a ubiquitous definition of childhood "creativity" that was a euphemism for control.

Thinking back to my years as an elementary art teacher, I realize how classroom activities reflected a lifeless methodology that betrayed the true and fundamental power of art—its ability to transform us into thinking, caring human beings. It's not that I was a bad teacher, but because of all of the control, art class was less than it could have been. I censored students and myself. Not surprisingly, I denied or ignored the students' lives. I rendered invisible important issues. I noticed that students' conversations about art were facile. I became alarmed that I was fostering educational dependency in them. "What do you want?" they would ask me. "Is this okay?"

EXPANDING NOTIONS OF TEACHER: ALLOWING STUDENT AGENCY AND VOICE

Allowing student agency required my rethinking the roles of teacher and student. Freire's (1990) "problem-posing" model for education focused my energies on student-generated learning. My role as teacher became much more advisory as I "permitted" the sharing of responsibility for our intellectual environment. Students' interests, life experiences, and knowledge began to form the backbone of the curriculum.

It was Mary Belenky et al.'s (1986) "midwife" teaching model that offered me the insight I needed to assist students rather than lead them. Their concepts of sharing, connecting, and cooperating guided me as I reconsidered my role as teacher/facilitator. By considering students as active agents in their education, I transformed my teaching. Demystifying a once objective learning process revealed to them and me new levels of subjective understanding.

Although such a notion of teaching might seem like heresy to some, I perceived it as a return to sanity. It felt like "coming home." It confirmed for me that "good teaching" is about complexity where power, history, community, agency, and identity converge.[1] It has only been within the past few years, however, that I have developed the confidence to enjoy my teaching.

EXPERIMENTS IN EDUCATION: RETHINKING THEORY INTO NEW PRACTICES

Returning to graduate school (1989–1996) allowed me to experiment with alternative pedagogical practices. I developed a ten-hour workshop in conjunction with College for Kids. College for Kids familiarizes gifted and highly motivated fourth through sixth graders with higher-education opportunities. Selected students spend three weeks on campus engaged in one-week workshops mentored by a supervising teacher who simultaneously earns graduate credit.

Preparation for my workshop began a half-year in advance and consisted of developing a title and course description. I chose Art and Social Change: From the Simpsons through the Gulf War to the Olympics. I decided to engage students in contemporary issues—in short, what we do at the university. I was purposefully vague in the course description in order to allow the topics to emerge from the students.

As the workshop drew near, I became wary of my approach. No other teachers had planned their sessions this way. Apart from declaring a general theme of art and social change, students would make the decisions. Years of university training and classroom teaching had not prepared me for the self-doubt I experienced prior to the workshop.[2]

Day One: Creating Community

At our first two-hour session, I explained the format of the class: students would create, collaborate, and support one another. We discussed contemporary social issues, looked at slides and books, and talked about possible projects. Students seemed as interested in my opinions about art as I was in theirs.

Days Two Through Four: Community in Action

Three different groups developed. One group of two students focused on technology and portraiture. They used scanners and digital cameras to examine issues of isolation. Another group of two developed a comic book based on discrimination issues. A third group of six, intrigued with recent cultural events concerning athletes, particularly those surrounding O. J. Simpson, decided to produce a video. Using Should Athletes Be Role Models? as a theme, they interviewed one another on tape. To prepare for their interviews, they planned a research timetable. Each member selected a task: researcher, writer, actor, or technician. This group isolated itself in an adjacent seminar room. The supervising teacher broached their request for secrecy. She insisted she be permitted into the room to monitor progress periodically. I chose instead to honor their request.

All three groups worked diligently and completed their projects. Unlike in previous lessons that I had taught, I found time to witness students' learning. I enjoyed my role as facilitator. Teaching was less hectic, and I got to know the students.

Day Five: Presenting Process and Product

On the last day of the workshop we invited another class and presented our projects to one another. Groups discussed not only their products but the thinking behind them as well. Such testimonies are an important part of a connected model. The portrait group spoke about portraits as living images. The comic book group explained the background of their project: a storekeeper had asked them to leave a comic book store because he perceived them as "kids fingering products" with no intent to purchase. The video group previewed their six-minute tape. They focused on creative and technical difficulties and addressed the anxieties and pleasures of working as a group.

Students evaluated their workshop experience with medium to high marks. The experience seemed more like real life than school. The supervising teacher, on the other hand, criticized my classroom management style. A good teacher, she noted, was one that was on top of everything, in charge and in control. But her reactions belied the reality of the class: there were no discipline problems, and students engaged in their work.

CONNECTED TEACHING AT THE UNIVERSITY LEVEL

I have incorporated aspects of connected teaching into my university teaching. In one of my art education courses students signed up to give historical presentations from Foster Wygant's (1993) *School Art in American Culture: 1820–1970*. Students chose book chapters that paralleled their interests. One group presented a chronological survey of schools and art in the nineteenth century. They augmented their presentation with family photographs, slides, and books. After the presentation they described difficulties they had experienced in locating information. That frank discussion convinced students that it was okay to help one another.

The 1946–1959 group focused on Black Mountain College and the social issues of the cold war.[3] They invited students to dress to the time period. They transformed the art room into a 1950s coffeehouse replete with coffee tables, table cloths, the smell of coffee, and burning candles. A slide timer enabled continuous projection of slides of artists on one wall. They even had us participate in a civil defense drill. Such drills were choreographed group performances in the 1950s and 1960s that prepared us to protect ourselves in public schools against nuclear attacks. A typical drill consisted of proceeding to basement areas and lining up against walls with our hands over our heads or simply hiding under our desks for (maximum) protection.

Gradually students' attitudes toward learning changed. They valued the experiences as well as the class itself. The experience marked a turning point in their course work. They witnessed an educational approach that was validating and supportive. Connecting art to their lives was difficult but well worth the struggle.

INTEGRATING STUDENTS' LIVES
INTO THE CURRICULUM

In another foundations course I had similar reactions integrating students' interests and lives into the course material. Some students helped co-plan certain aspects of the course. For example, some students brought readings. We listened to one another. Themes—our hopes, fears, expectations, experiences, and desires—became avenues to engage art and education. Such examinations helped us discover not only our own but also one another's humanity. Final presentations represented how students internalized such personal approaches.

One student narrated a slide presentation explaining how he and his family cared for his younger hemophiliac brother. Slides revealed a nurturing brother assisting in life-care. Most students were silent throughout his presentation. Some cried.

Another student shared with us her reawakening to her Hispanic heritage. She explained how the class discussions energized her, and she began to reexamine her "roots." Although apologetic for not knowing more about her race or ethnicity, she determined to learn more.

Still another student spoke about childhood abuse. She shared her journey of understanding her relationship to her own history of abuse. She described how euphoric yet frightened she felt in choosing a topic that had personal meaning.

Another moving moment occurred when one student showed slides of her institutionalized grandfather. She documented his life with Alzheimer's disease. Both music and slides represented her struggle: losing someone she loved. Male and female students were in tears throughout her presentation.

SELF-CONNECTING AND SELF-EDUCATION

> *I think that what we need are more complicated*
> *ways of imagining ourselves in the world that*
> *are truer to what people know and what peo-*
> *ple's imaginations are about.*
>   HERMAN GRAY IN M. T. RIGGS, 1991

Like the many students I observe daily in schools or interact with in university settings, I entered school with certain race, class, and gender experiences. Unfortunately, I was unable to integrate much of my personal life into my art. This was true even at the graduate level. Teachers treated me as a passive consumer. In many ways teachers prevented me from experiencing truly transforming art experiences. In retrospect I see that I perpetuated such an ideology of "screening"—shielding students from the real world, further marginalizing art in the classroom.

My experience teaching in schools compels me to question art practices that reconstitute art into a "safe" subject. As we sanitize art and reduce it to inane elements, we need to ask ourselves: Is this art education? What are we perpetuating? Students know what is truthful and real to them. We need to validate their ideas about art through their lives. By controlling students, we deny everybody the opportunity to experience the transforming effects of art.

It takes great personal courage for me to publicly *rethink* how I teach in a classroom. To move from a controlling pedagogy to one that is more student centered and joy filled is to constantly confront my own demons: the bored and boring tradition that I now reject. Yet, as I spiral through my own learning, I remind myself that boredom itself was key to my pedagogical shift. Such a recognition allows me to further let go of control, yet look within the traditions of art and education for other ways to learn and teach.

Teachers can already create spaces in classrooms where creativity, imagination, and critical thinking are more apt to occur, and it is already possible to rethink teaching. These teachers let go of false personae (of authority or truth, for example) and let their real selves and the real world into their art and classrooms. Inviting the real world into the classroom entails real emotions, real problems, real art, real artists—initial results: excitement and voice. Both my boredom and my search were roads to better teaching: roads on which I enable not only students' creativity but my own; roads on which we together reexamine, share, and release power.

NOTES

[1]Relationships between power and knowledge have been scrutinized for some time now (Apple, 1979, 1982; Bourdieu, 1984; Dalton, 1995; Duncum, 1989; Silin, 1995; Wolff, 1981). Dalton (1995) laments that "most contemporary art education theories continue to be trapped within the discourses of the high Modernism of the thirties and forties" (p. 45). Although art educators have argued for curricular reform (Beyer, 1984; Brady, 1986; Duncum, 1989; King, 1987; Perr, 1988; Schellin, 1990), resistance to change remains steadfast. For example, Cahan and Kocur's (1996) curriculum text espouses critical perspectives and runs counter to much art education discourse that continues to focus on interpretations and reinterpretations of modernist principles and practices (see Anderson & McRorie, 1997).

[2]In this case, anxiety was a good thing in that it honored my uneasiness as I ventured onto unfamiliar pedagogical terrain.

[3]This group of students presented a version of their presentation at the 1997 Texas Art Education Association fall convention.

REFERENCES

Anderson, T., & McRorie, S. (1997). A role for aesthetics in centering the K–12 art curriculum. *Art Education, 50* (3), 6–14.

Apple, M. (1979). *Ideology and curriculum.* New York: Routledge.

————. (1982). *Education and power.* New York: Routledge.

Belenky, M., Clinchy, B., Mattuck, J., & Tarule, N. (1986). *Women's ways of knowing: The development of self, voice and mind.* New York: Basic Books.

Beyer, L. E. (1984). The arts, school practice, and cultural transformation. *Bulletin of the Caucus on Social Theory and Art Education, 4,* 1–13.

Bourdieu, P. (1984). *Distinction: A social critique of the judgment of taste.* R. Nice, trans. Cambridge, MA: Harvard University Press.

Brady, P. (1986). Art, excellence and a liberal education. *Journal of the Institute of Art Education, 10* (3), 56–63.

Cahan, S., & Kocur, Z. (1996). *Contemporary art and multicultural education.* New York: Routledge.

Dalton, P. (1995). Modernism, art education and sexual difference. In K. Deepwell, ed., *New feminist art criticism: Critical strategies* (pp. 44–50). New York: St. Martin's.

Duncum, P. (1989). Toward foundations for a socially critical art education. *Journal of Social Theory in Art Education, 9,* 12–25.

Efland, A. (1976). The school art style: A functional analysis. *Studies in Art Education, 17* (2), 37–44.

Freire, P. (1990). *Pedagogy of the oppressed.* New York: Continuum.

Giroux, H. (1994). Borderline artists, cultural workers, and the crisis of democracy. In C. Becker & A. Wiens, eds., *The artist in society: Rights, roles and responsibilities* (pp. 4–14). Chicago: New Art Examiner Press.

King, G. (1987). The laundering of art: Where have all the issues gone? *Journal of the Institute of Art Education, 11* (1), 37–41.

Perr, H. (1988). *Making art together: Step-by-step.* San Jose, CA: Resource Publications.

Riggs, M. T., director and producer. (1991). *Color adjustment* (documentary video). Stanford, CA: Signifyin' Works.

Schellin, P. (1990). Art education in the time of AIDS. *Journal of Social Theory in Art Education, 10,* 83–93.

Silin, J. (1995). *Sex, death, and the education of children: Our passion for ignorance in the age of AIDS.* New York: Teachers College Press.

Wachowiak, F. (1977). *Emphasis art: A qualitative art program for the elementary school* (3rd ed.). New York: Thomas Y. Crowell.

Wolff, J. (1981). *The social production of art.* New York: New York University Press.

Wygant, F. (1993). *School art in American culture: 1820–1970.* Cincinnati, OH: Interwood.

CHAPTER 17

Going Nowhere: Exploring the Cyberspace Between Our Ears

MICHAEL J. EMME

When you look in your mirror, how do you feel about what you see? If you are like me, the honest answer is: Sometimes good, sometimes not so good. As I inventory errant and cooperative hairs, regional and seasonal skin variations, and the aesthetics of my face in general, I am using basic technology—a mirror—to extend my perception. The facts of my face combine with my memories and aspirations to produce my self-image.

Over the centuries technological advances—glass lenses, lasers, and now computers—have extended our perceptions. These advances gave us new eyes that do the same things our old eyes did—accumulate fragments from which we construct worldviews—but these new eyes have millions of sockets, and the massive amounts of mass media surrounding us order the accumulation to a substantive degree.

Computer technology is changing traditional understandings of perception, in which the metaphor of the lens dominates (Crary, 1992). Like lenses, computers also extend our sight, but unlike lenses, computers extend more. By combining auditory and visual technologies with interactivity, computers give us digitally enhanced, three- and four-dimensional perceptions. This makes cyberspace, like our bodies and our environments, better understood as a place than as a picture.

To "get" the messy interactivity of cyberspace, we need to comprehend its metaphors of place and architecture. Cyberspace at times resembles a murky bus depot where chance encounters, tantalizing glimpses, and adrenalized promise create unmet desires. As we cross into unfamiliar territory (Giroux, 1988), we need wise and creative strategies for making meaningful and safe selections from wildly divergent possibilities.

In this chapter I explore how art education can contribute to a creative and wise use of the worlds of cyberspace. Teaching in cyberspace involves adapting our perceptions of time, place, and memory and questioning the value of linear, traditional, and, at times, even rational thinking.

From our first awareness that "the little kid in the mirror is me!" to the full bloom of our personal identities (again, shaped in part by the media), visual technologies constantly influence us. For the last half millennium, our minds and intelligence have been understood to be like books. Today we compare our minds to computers (Bolter, 1984). These metaphors impact how we think about ourselves, how we educate, and how we learn.

SIMULTANEITY AND THE THREE-DIMENSIONAL MIND

Much contemporary art theory (Crary, 1992; Solso, 1994; Stafford, 1993, 1994, 1996) concerns the delightful dances between memory and vision. In *Postmodern Geographies* (1989) Edward Soja states, "It may be space more than time that hides consequences from us, the 'making of geography' more than the 'making of history' that provides the most revealing tactical and theoretical world" (p. 1). Soja and other contemporary theorists suggest that our minds and social structures be understood in three-dimensional terms. Soja suggests that simultaneous and juxtaposed mixtures of past and present in this three-dimensional worldview differentiate modernity and postmodernity. Linear narrative cannot express the complexity of postmodernity. Soja (1989) cites Foucault:

> The great obsession of the nineteenth century was, as we know, history: with its themes of development and suspension, of crisis and cycle, themes of the ever-accumulating past, with its great preponderance of dead men and the menacing glaciation of the world. . . . The present epoch will perhaps above all be the epoch of space. We are in the epoch of simultaneity: we are in the epoch of juxtaposition, the epoch of the near and far, of the side-by-side, of the dispersed. (P. 10)

In our daily experience simultaneity is the pang of conscience we feel slipping into our new Nikes as we remember the inhumane conditions of their manufacture. It is also the awareness of joining other Nike wearers as we lace up. Built on mass-mediated memory, this Nike experience emerges as a complex, communal construct that in turn creates global conceptual architecture.

In exploring memory in relation to architecture, Malcolm Quantrill (1987) suggests that a building is not only an artifact of the past, but that it also functions for contemporary viewers as a framework for new memories. Similarly, Renaissance how-to manuals used architectural imagery to remember stories (Willis 1621/1973). Having visualized a building with many rooms, a storyteller was instructed to mentally deposit parts of a story in each room. When it came time to retell the story, the storyteller would mentally walk to each room and pick up the needed details of the story. Such mnemonic strategies demonstrate our capacity to think both spatially and visually. As every politician and university chancellor with a brass plaque on the side of a building knows, architecture also serves as a primary example of extrapsychic memory (Strømnes, 1980, p. 27). Psychological research supports the notion that we think in images, that "the visual" is central to human symbolic communication:

> Although we recognize by means of all our senses, we typically recall sights and sounds more easily than smells, tastes, and feels. We can represent visual and acoustic images easily to ourselves, while this is more difficult with the other senses. Our ability to recall and fantasize in spatial and acoustic images (even imagining our own minds as "places" containing "ghosts" and "memories") shows that sensory memory of space and sound is no less conceptual than is our abstract memory of meanings. (Fentress & Wickham, 1992, pp. 30–31)

In *Remembering Postmodernism* Mark Cheetham (1991) describes the relationship between artist and audience as memories engaging in the political business of constructing meaning. In our time of increasing exposure to visual and other information, that which makes its way into our memories impacts how we construct our perceptions. When Rosalind Krauss (1985) described the camera as a prosthetic device, she provided an apt metaphor for how technology allows us first to see more, and then to see the inadequacies of our physiological tools of perception. This dissatisfaction with our biological limits is key to understanding the significance of technology—our new eyes.

In the "The Value of Going Nowhere," Jason Greenburg (1996, p. 25) describes virtual reality as "nonspace" and "nonexistence." He accepts computer-generated reality as real and worries about those who have access only to physical space. Will our world's technologically driven transformation of perception create a class of "the perceptually impaired"? How far along are we in shifting our memories and perceptions into mass-media cyberspace? And which students are being left behind?

SELF-SCULPTURE ON THE INTERNET

North Americans who do not suffer from TV paranoia may be aware of the many utopic iterations of *Star Trek*. One recurring character archetype is the Borg. Referred to as a collective, the Borg are individuals who are electronically linked such that they function as one mind. Each individual, encrusted with electronic and mechanical prosthetics, can access the memories and knowledge of the entire collective. Borg cannot think individually, since individual thoughts become part of the collective's memory. In one story line *Star Trek* crew members zealously forced an individual Borg, isolated from the collective, to return to her preassimilation individuality. In "The Art of Cyberspace," Pierre Levy (1996) refers to cyberspace as a collective, but his vision is of cacophony creating symphony:

> Utilizing all the resources cyberspace offers, the art of involvement discovers the current of music. How do we make a symphony rise from the murmur of a multiple? How do we transform the sound of a crowd into a chorus, without a musical score? The collective intellect continually brings the social contract into play, it keeps the group in a state of renewal. . . . To do so requires time, the time to involve individuals, to form ties, to make objects appear, and create common landscapes and to return to them. In comparison to the watch or the calendar, the temporality of the [cyber-]collective imagination may seem delayed, interrupted, splintered. Yet it is all played out in the dark, invisible recesses of the collective: the melody, the emotional tonality, the secret pulse, the connections, and continuity that it binds together at the very heart of the individuals of which it is composed. (p. 397)

Internet chat rooms exemplify this. In a chat room gentle, intimate conversations intermingle with sexual aggression, racist invective, and bursts of anger reminiscent of Tourette's syndrome. Chat room navigators experience the simultaneity of cyberspace—it is simultaneously private and public, safe and dangerous.

While Levy defines cyberspace as a place of interaction, it is also, like all communication environments, a place of representation. Now please join me in a game of self-sculpture. If you accept that we think visually and spatially, and that cyberspace is a place, then it makes sense that we should be able to describe cyberspace and its inhabitants in architectural terms and fabricate three- or even four-dimensional self-portraits. Your building materials include your own input as well as limitless data from cyberspace. To begin, list several words that describe yourself. These can include age, gender, race, beliefs, hobbies, art preferences, phobias, hair color, complexion, and so on. Don't include anything unless it represents some aspect of yourself. Using an Internet search engine to search your descriptors, you will discover a picture that is both you and not you. You will discover whole audiences that desire your parts, industries that want to market to your specific ills, and agencies, both governmental and independent, that already have you in their databases. You will also find people who share similar life experiences, people who will give you their time in exchange for yours.

In doing this search, I discovered that as a male I am first of all a warrior, a Norse god, or an athlete. As a photographer I am concerned with having my work in collections and invested in the exchange of erotica, before I even begin to think about the wider sense of my medium. As a parent I am part of an enormous collective that is largely female. My hands are for tool use but are also powerful Christian, Islamic, and mystical symbols. My freckles, big chin, and curly hair are both fetish objects and problems that I can solve with the right treatment. This sculpture can be as elaborate or simplistic as you choose. It will change from day to day, and no matter how hard you try, it will be you and not you. In a world where information has value, where access codes, bar codes, and account numbers are considered more reliable identification than your body, pattern is displacing presence (Hayles, 1996).

THE VIRTUAL ARCHITECTURE OF THE INTERNET

By choosing *Frozen Music* as the title of their text on the architecture of Portland, Oregon, Gideon Bosker and Lena Lencek (1985) created a metaphor for connecting patterns in music and architecture. This metaphor, while apt, is static. It asks us to see a building's facade as sheet music. This metaphor makes me want to run a black-and-white photograph of an interesting building across the laser scanner at a local grocery store so that I can hear the building. This wish focuses on the relationship between listening to music and moving one's gaze across a building's facade.

An expansion of Bosker and Lencek's metaphor could compare moving through a building with the experience of the divergences, pauses, and simultaneity of some of John Cage's musical environments. The notion of technology impacting our construction of pattern is at the core of this metaphor. Each chosen path defines a pattern. Therefore, our discoveries are the product, while the viability of any particular pattern validates our process. Each walk through the building offers an experience different from prior experiences without invalidating the prior experiences.

For art educators considering the educational challenges and opportunities posed by computers, the Internet, and the World Wide Web, the questions are not: What's the content? How do I teach this? Rather, they are: What can we bring from art into cyberspace? How can the tools we know function in cyberspace? How will cyberspace change our tools, our perceptions, and our art? Abundant, floridly written, futurist articles that "predict" the effects of cyberspace consider such questions of human development and social interaction. Part of the business of art making is to explore such issues and, as with all phenomena, make meaning as we go.

Art offers many means for moving through, manipulating, and making art in space. Yet introductory design texts typically emphasize two-dimensional experience. Art history, as experienced in the classroom, foregrounds two-dimensionality to the point of framing three-dimensional work in two dimensions (Roberts, 1995). Visionary art educators can help students respond to the immersive environments of cyberspace. If teachers include both physical and conceptual three-dimensionality in their curriculum, students can learn strategies for working in space and time as environments, to create an architecture that can encompass objects, installation work, and performance art, all of which are interactive, nonlinear environments.

In *Sociology's Emotions* (1997) Ann Game refers to the rationalist notion that objective distance is always preferable to emotional engagement. In art we claim emotional engagement with artworks; yet the language of aesthetics reveals that our engagement remains framed by rationalist traditions. To teach art meaningfully today, we need to create comfort in our students with concepts such as simultaneity, subjectivity, relativity, three- and four-dimensionality, virtual reality, and cyberspace. We need to expand on portfolio assessment literature that emphasizes process over product, because in a cyberenvironment work is judged on its feasibility as much as its correctness (Rodin, 1993, p. xv). In the end, we and our students not only must understand the nowhere of cyberspace as somewhere, but we must also become agile with the cyberspace between our ears.

REFERENCES

Bolter, J. D. (1984). *Turing's man: Western culture in the computer age.* Chapel Hill: University of North Carolina Press.

Bosker, G., & Lencek, L. (1985). *Frozen music: A history of Portland architecture.* Portland: Oregon Historical Society.

Cheetham, M. (1991). *Remembering postmodernism: Trends in recent Canadian art.* Toronto: Oxford University Press.

Crary, J. (1992). *Techniques of the observer: On vision and modernity in the nineteenth century.* Cambridge, MA: MIT Press.

Fentress, J., & Wickham, C. (1992). *Social memory: New perspectives on the past.* Oxford, UK: Blackwell.

Game, A. (1997). Sociology's emotions. *Canadian Review of Sociology and Anthropology, 34* (4), 385–400.

Giroux, H. (1988). Border pedagogy in the age of postmodern. *Journal of Education, 179* (3), 162–181.

Greenburg, J. (1996). The value of going nowhere: A tale of virtual existence. *New Art Examiner, 24* (1), 24–30.

Hayles, N. K. (1996). Virtual bodies and flickering signifiers. In T. Duckery, ed., *Electronic cultures: Technology and visual representation* (pp. 259–277). Denville, NJ: Aperture Foundation.

Krauss, R. (1985). *L'Amour fou: Photography and surrealism.* New York: Corcoran Gallery, Abbeville.

Levy, P. (1996). The art of cyberspace. K. Lundell, trans. In T. Duckery, ed., *Electronic cultures: Technology and representation* (pp. 396–397). Denville, NJ: Aperture Foundation.

Quantrill, M. (1987). *The environmental memory: Man and architecture in the landscape of ideas.* New York: Shocken.

Roberts, H. (1995). *Art history through the lens of a camera.* Amsterdam: OPA.

Rodin, E. (1993). Foreword. In M. Emmer, ed., *The visual mind, art, and mathematics.* Cambridge, MA: MIT Press.

Soja, E. (1989). *Postmodern geographies: The reassertion of space in critical theory.* New York: Verso.

Solso, R. L. (1994). *Cognition and the visual arts.* Cambridge, MA: MIT Press.

Stafford, B. M. (1993). *Body criticism: Imaging the unseen in enlightenment art and medicine.* Cambridge, MA: MIT Press.

————. (1994). *Artful science: Enlightenment entertainment and the eclipse of visual education.* Cambridge, MA: MIT Press.

————. (1996). *Good looking: The virtue of images.* Cambridge, MA: MIT Press.

Strømnes, F. (1980). On the architecture of thought. *Abacus,* 27–29.

Willis, J. (1621). *The art of memory.* Facsimile, 1973. Amsterdam: Da Capo Press.

CHAPTER 18

By the People: A Community-Based Art Curriculum

KAREN KEIFER-BOYD

In 1989 Oregon's McKenzie River valley community members met in a historic landmark, the state's oldest fish hatchery, to discuss art education for the children who lived within the forty-mile range of the Mc-Kenzie school district. At the time, I was a parent, an art teacher, a community member, a graduate student, and on this evening, the facilitator of the meeting.

To distribute the meeting announcements, my five-year-old son, Calder, his seven-year-old brother, Ovid, and I had driven forty miles along the McKenzie Highway, at first stopping at every newspaper box and shop. After two hours we began to place the announcements only in newspaper boxes next to decorated mailboxes. I rationalized that people who decorated their mailboxes would be more likely to participate in aesthetic-expressive discourse. Calder and Ovid placed one hundred flyers that day, thus beginning a community-wide, consensus-building, participatory project to develop a K–6 art curriculum for our rural school district.

Our tasks were to develop goals, guidelines, and content. The first step was to identify local resources, aesthetic values, needs, and interests. The second was to identify connections between the community's art educational concerns and its aesthetic practices. The third was to develop strategies based on the information generated in the first two steps.

Consensus decision making works best when participants respect one another and express diverse perspectives. The participants in our group listened to one another and articulated various views, and we reached a consensus.

Specific strategies helped me to facilitate the six-month consensus process to build an art curriculum. These included relinquishing my control as leader and embracing group dynamics. When enacted locally, this participatory approach can replace a dominant culture's homogenous aesthetic practices by celebrating the vibrant aesthetic energy found within a specific community.

Rejecting a dualistic, "win/lose" approach to conflict solving, the different groups (i.e., teachers, administrators, students, and community members) created alternatives that incorporated all participants' concerns. This approach prevents adhering to universalized standards. Grounded in postmodern social theory—in this case, a rejection of grand narratives of art—this approach instead derives meaning from local experiences, traditions, and beliefs. Postmodern theorists "offer indeterminacy rather than determinism, diversity rather than synthesis, complexity rather than simplification" (Rosenau, 1992, p. 8).

Benefits of an art curriculum "suited to the site" include maximizing local resources, developing pride in a community's cultural heritage, creating support for art education, and connecting art with local culture. In a community-based art curriculum, art becomes meaningful to students because their art lessons encourage pride rather than neglect toward their own aesthetic values. Students compare their aesthetic values with those of a diversity of other cultures. In short, culture is localized, not imported.

Since 1990 Oregon has undergone an economic downturn that has impacted education funding. We designed the McKenzie River art curriculum to respond to socioeconomic shifts. In this chapter I discuss four factors that contributed to its success. I also discuss the facilitator's role, the social theory underlying our approach, and how flexibility in an art curriculum can promote ongoing community support for it. My 1989 master's thesis, "A Case Study and Theoretical Analysis of a Participatory Process to Develop an Art Curriculum for Grades K–6"—supplemented with follow-up interviews with teachers, students, administrators, and community members—provided the material for this chapter.

FOUR FACTORS THAT CONTRIBUTED TO THE SUCCESS OF THE MCKENZIE RIVER ART CURRICULUM PROJECT

In 1990 Oregon's educational accreditation board designated the McKenzie art curriculum an outstanding model of art education. Four factors contributed substantively to the project's success: selling the idea of a site-specific art curriculum, developing community networks, separating idea generation from idea evaluation, and incorporating community participation.

Success Factor One: Sell the Idea of a Site-Specific Art Curriculum

To initiate the project, I provided information to the school and school district decision makers about the costs and benefits of adopting nationally distributed art textbooks and curricula. I then compared that option to their participation in creating a site-specific art curriculum guided by an art education specialist. The ways art curricula are developed, and the forms in which art lessons are packaged, relate to philosophical position, content, and teaching practice. Teaching art from a nationally distributed, permanently bound textbook tends to "bind" users to a standardized and uniform view of art and art education. Developing a community-based art curriculum validates diversity and contextualism. A curriculum that can be altered on a computer according to annual evaluations and a changing teacher pool can reflect the diversity and dynamism of art and life. Electronically alterable art lessons are less costly to update and revise than a bound textbook, and now curriculum writers have use of the Internet's extensive resources to supplement and modify their materials.

Success Factor Two: Develop Communication Networks

Utilize art education specialists as facilitators and resources. The specialist's role is not one of control or even necessarily expertise in local needs and aesthetic preferences. It consists instead of opening communication channels, gathering information, seeking emergent patterns, and presenting options. Participatory processes establish communication among people who formerly had no way to voice opinions to those outside their own sphere. An environment that is neither threatening nor antagonistic will facilitate dialogue. A cooperative environment arises when all participants' concerns are acknowledged and discussed respectfully.

Success Factor Three: Separate Idea Generation from Idea Evaluation

A facilitator of a participatory process needs to separate idea generation from idea evaluation. A facilitator gains participants' trust, provides art educational expertise, and coordinates the accomplishment of creative revisions throughout the process.

Group processes such as the Nominal Group Technique, interactive brainstorming, and the Delphi approach are effective means to explore problems and create solutions. Group process techniques emphasize either information formation and evaluation or social/personal forces in their application. For example, the Nominal Group Technique (NGT), developed by Delbecq and Van de Ven in 1968, focuses on information handling. NGT has strict guidelines concerning collecting and evaluating information, developing alternative courses of action, and choosing a direction (Delbecq, Van de Ven, & Gustafson, 1975). I used a modified version of NGT for this project. I first asked teachers to generate ideas in writing using a questionnaire format, and then followed this with a round-robin feedback session in which the teachers clarified, evaluated, and prioritized their suggestions.

Interactive brainstorming involves nonjudgmentally collecting many ideas and then expanding on them. I encouraged the participants to be impartial and not voice opinions during the idea-generating phase.

In the Delphi approach participants do not meet in person but communicate through written exercises. A key aspect of the Delphi Technique that we used in the McKenzie River project was that each member assumed the role of critical evaluator. Before the participants began their week-long efforts to develop their ideas, however, I discussed the questionnaire's purpose and demonstrated some possibilities. Then I gave teachers a summary of all responses, including ideas from the community. This avoided individual inhibitions and premature evaluations while it enhanced idea generation.

Irving Janis's (1972) "groupthink" theory resulted from analyzing social-psychological forces in group decision making. From his study of situations in which experts made poor decisions, Janis developed a strategy to help groups avoid groupthink. Groupthink occurs when one position achieves dominance too early and limits other possibilities. By assigning several groups the same tasks, I avoided insulation of an in-group. At intervals we connected our ideas and sought outside challenges. After reaching a preliminary consensus on the curriculum, we reexamined it prior to forming a final consensus.

Success Factor Four: Participation Breeds Support and Commitment

A group will accept a decision more readily if it participates in making the decision. According to Paulo Freire (1990), an internationally recognized educator and human rights activist, "to alienate [people] from their own decision-making is to change them into objects" (p. 73). He added this further observation: "Many political and educational plans have failed because their authors designed them according to their own personal views of reality, never once taking into account (except as mere objects of the action) the *[people]-in-a situation* to whom their program was ostensibly directed" (p. 83). In a participatory process the community decides what will affect them and their children. This builds support and enthusiasm among teachers, administrators, parents, students, and other community members. This was evinced by the time, money, and space the McKenzie River community gave to its art program.

FACILITATING COMMUNITY DECISION MAKING FOR DEVELOPING OUR ART CURRICULUM

Developing our community-based curriculum involved nine distinct steps that we followed between January and June of 1989:

1. Conducting a pilot program
2. Presenting alternatives
3. Using a questionnaire
4. Facilitating brainstorming sessions
5. Merging ideas
6. Critiquing ideas
7. Compiling critiques
8. Revisiting ideas and their critiques
9. Presenting the finished curriculum to the school board and community

In step eight, teachers reached consensus on the McKenzie art curriculum's goals, guidelines, and format. From these guidelines I prepared art lessons, helped teachers to teach them, and worked with teachers to evaluate and revise them through the fall and into the spring of 1990.

Step One: The Pilot Program

I conducted a pilot program in which I worked individually with each teacher to plan, organize, implement, and evaluate an art lesson. These lessons were based on teachers' selection of a country for their students to study. The lessons demonstrated the value of visual thinking to students and teachers, and an exhibit of works from the pilot lessons generated community interest.

Step Two: Alternative Choices

I presented alternatives to the core decision makers about investing in a participatory process or adopting an existing curriculum. We evaluated current art textbooks and teaching aids, explored controversies and trends in the field, and examined state, district, and school standards for art education. In 1989 national art education standards did not exist, but they do today and they would need to be included.

I informed the decision makers about local resources for teaching the community's unique heritage and provided a timeline for developing a site-specific art curriculum. The group then used a round-robin approach, with each member identifying negative and positive consequences of the two alternatives. I handwrote their comments on large paper for the group to discuss. I also audiotaped the discussion for later transcription onto a form from which the decision makers privately selected from the options.

At a subsequent meeting I presented the vote tallies, and then we used an organic webbing technique to discuss concerns and how to resolve them. The core decision makers unanimously selected the site-specific art curriculum. The tasks then were to establish priorities, determine sequence, schedule timing, and plan evaluation.

Step Three: The Teacher Questionnaire

Teachers attended a session to give their input on structuring the curriculum. After reviewing the curricular materials, they recorded this information on a questionnaire:

1. Descriptions of the art they currently were teaching.
2. Their definitions of art.
3. Their preferred frequency and length for art sessions.
4. Their rationales for art education.
5. Their evaluations of the pilot program.
6. The sequence of units in other subjects.
7. Their preferred areas of emphasis for art (assessed from a checklist of concepts, beliefs, values, objectives, content, and aesthetic and critical concerns, with room for additional responses).

8. Their curriculum formatting preferences determined from a checklist of options. (Respondents could select formats such as those exhibited at the meeting or alternatives and combinations.)

I combined the information from the questionnaires into a report and distributed it to the teachers.

Step Four: Brainstorming Sessions

I invited community members to discuss our art curriculum goals. Informal conversation occurred during various community gatherings I attended, and more structured dialogue occurred at a special community meeting to discuss the value of art, what children should learn about art, and local resources. I compiled the community's responses into a report. I also gathered student input on these three topics, emphasizing what types of art they would like to explore. I joined the children at their lunch tables, each lunch period visiting with a different class, until I had heard from each class.

Step Five: Idea Patterns

I coded data and identified emergent frequency patterns from the teacher questionnaires, the student lunch conversations, and the community meetings. From this analysis I developed goals, sequentialized subgoals by grade, and created a mock-up teacher's guide and a lesson plan format.

Step Six: Critiques

At a faculty meeting I presented the proposed goals and guidelines to teachers and administrators and facilitated a critique. I used Janis's strategy to avoid groupthink during the critique.

Step Seven: Critique Patterns

After compiling the responses to the critique, I looked for patterns and made changes based on the responses. In some situations I had to find alternatives to incorporate everyone's concerns. I then prepared a letter to the teachers in which I listed the responses and described the changes. I included a preliminary approval form for teachers to sign if they agreed with the goals, guidelines, and format of the curriculum.

Step Eight: Reviewing and Deciding

Teachers reviewed changes and signed their names if they approved of the goals, guidelines, and other components of the art program. Their unanimous approval permitted me to prepare eight fall art lessons per grade during the summer months. After a fall in-service, and after teachers practiced teaching the lessons, I met with each grade level's teachers to evaluate the lessons and plan the winter and spring art lessons. At the end of the school year the teachers and principal evaluated the program, goals, and guidelines.

Step Nine: Publicizing Art Curriculum Goals and Guidelines

By participating in the curriculum, local artists developed appreciation in students and other community members for local aesthetics and art-making practices. With the help of a local fiber artist and blues singer, third graders spun sheep's wool from a nearby ranch, dyed the wool with native plants found near the school, and wove a functional artwork. The artist taught the students to interpret the weaving's visual composition as music and to critique it according to blues rhythms.

Another community artist taught students to paint outdoor landscapes with watercolors. A quilting group helped with a fifth-grade quilt project that depicted events from U.S. history. Students watched a video, *Hearts and Hands* (Ferraro, 1987), which presented a history of the United States as recorded in quilts. The students raffled their quilt to support their one-week "outdoor school" experience (a tradition in many Oregon schools in which fifth graders spend a week in the mountains involved in environmental science and art activities). The school district showed support for the art program by financially compensating the community artists.

Administrative support also emerged when the elementary school principal and I presented the new art curriculum to the school board and the community. The superintendent responded with a note that read in part: "I found your presentation informative and educational. I especially liked the way you communicated art as a medium of reflecting movements and changes within societies" (E. Curtis, June 19, 1989).

SOCIAL THEORY IN A CONTEXT-DEPENDENT ART CURRICULUM

In 1975 Paul Feyerabend asserted that in a free society all traditions have equal rights and equal access to power. Postmodern social theorists also deal with this issue: "Social theories are social stories, or narratives, that are intimately related to the pressing social issues of the day. Furthermore, they are oriented not only to better understanding those issues but also to having an impact on social outcomes. They are not driven by insular theoretical interests but by moral, political, and social concerns" (Ritzer, 1997, p. 13). Social theory in a context-dependent art curriculum involves the comparing of values and beliefs of diverse groups, particularly in terms of the sociopolitics from which their art forms arise. The curriculum does not privilege the arts of one group over others, thus preventing "valorizing certain perspectives and marginalizing others" (Ritzer, 1997, p. 4). The creators of the McKenzie River art curriculum embedded its content within local context.

TEN YEARS LATER

Developing and implementing the art curriculum required three years. In year one we planned and piloted, in year two we held in-services and modeled art lessons, and in year three we evaluated and revised. When in 1990 the state education accreditation team evaluated the McKenzie public school district, they acknowledged the art curriculum as one of the best in the state. At the time, Oregon required the adoption of approved textbooks for teaching art; however, the state made an exception and endorsed our curriculum as an alternative.

The school district needed a coordinator to keep the curriculum current. Oregon, however, does not budget for K–6 art education, and the 1991 passage of Measure 5 caused McKenzie's music, physical education, and library positions to be cut or reduced. Would our community-based art curriculum survive?

In the summer of 1998 I returned to McKenzie to interview the former principal (now a special education teacher at the school) and several faculty members who had participated in creating the curriculum. I also spoke with one teacher who joined the faculty after we had written the curriculum.

I learned that average class sizes had increased from eighteen to twenty-five students, with some as large as thirty-one students. Decreasing budgets have created a state accreditation process that neglects art education. Recent teacher in-services have focused on a new graduation requirement—certificates of initial and advanced mastery with no art requirements. These developments have seriously diminished art education in the McKenzie school district.

Community changes also have weakened the school district's art education. In 1989 many parents worked for the Forest Service, which encouraged employee volunteerism. Parents who in 1989 had been University of Oregon students or employed in various McKenzie River enterprises had supported the arts and pressured the district to include art education. By 1998 many of these families had moved elsewhere to find work. Today the community consists of an elderly population and young families laid off from the Forest Service. Many members of these two groups lack motivation to help at the schools or transportation to get there. Art education is no longer a community concern.

However, some of the curriculum's art lessons have developed into strong community traditions. The quilt project has become a major event for each fifth-grade class. One popular story tells of a grandmother who won the quilt the year her granddaughter's class created it and gave it to her granddaughter at her graduation. Each year the quilt has had different themes. In 1994 the theme was famous women in history, which stirred some local controversy. Another year the quilt's theme dealt with watershed environmental issues. Several lessons that integrated the environment and local aesthetics survived funding and administrative barriers. Some McKenzie classroom teachers became "secure in art" as a result of working on the curriculum, and they continue offering art lessons in their classes.

STRUCTURING FLEXIBILITY AND LOCAL RELEVANCY IN AN ART CURRICULUM

The curriculum can remain relevant primarily because of two built-in features: its annual curriculum assessment chart and its digital format. Those who teach and learn from it feel ownership in it because they participate in its evolution. They feel confident that they can adjust it to changing needs.

Ownership and commitment were the most beneficial features of the participatory process and the consensus decision making. However, lack of leadership and accountability for the curriculum by any of the district's constituencies—the community, state accreditors, teachers, or administrators—undermined some of the curriculum's positive energy. Nevertheless, its relevance and participatory approach made certain projects, such as the class quilt, into integral parts of the school's curriculum and the community's local aesthetic identity.

REFERENCES

Delbecq, A. L., Van de Ven, A. H., & Gustafson, D. H. (1975). *Group techniques for program planning: A guide to Nominal Group and Delphi processes.* Glenview, IL: Scott, Foresman.

Ferraro, P., producer/director, & Ferris, B., writer. (1987). *Hearts and hands* (videorecording). San Francisco, CA: Hearts and Hands Films. Distributed by Ferrero Films.

Feyerabend, P. (1975). *Science in a free society.* London: NLB.

Freire, P. (1990). *Pedagogy of the oppressed.* M. B. Ramos, trans. New York: Continuum.

Janis, I. L. (1972). *Victims of groupthink* (2nd ed.). Boston: Houghton Mifflin.

Keifer-Boyd, K. (1989). A case study and theoretical analysis of a participatory process to develop an art curriculum for grades K–6. Master's thesis, University of Oregon.

Ritzer, G. (1997). *Postmodern social theory.* New York: McGraw-Hill.

Rosenau, P. M. (1992). *Post-modernism and the social sciences: Insights, inroads, and intrusions.* Princeton, NJ: Princeton University Press.

Contributors

Future Akins
Artist, Art Instructor, 4715 27th Street, Lubbock, TX 79410
Hattiemay@aol.com

Ed Check
Assistant Professor of Art Education, Texas Tech University
P.O. Box 42081, Lubbock, TX 79409-2081
abech@ttacs.ttu.edu

Kathleen E. Connors
Professor, Southern Connecticut State University
Art Department, Earl Hall
501 Crescent Street, New Haven, CT 06515-6652
connors@scsu.ctstateu.edu

Elizabeth Manley Delacruz
Associate Professor of Art Education and Women's Studies
University of Illinois
118 Art and Design Building, Champaign, IL 61820
edelacru@uiuc.edu

Grace Deniston-Trochta
Assistant Professor, University of Wisconsin–Oshkosh
523 Arts and Communication Building
800 Algoma Boulevard, Oshkosh, WI 54901-8605
deniston@uwosh.edu

Paul Duncum
Doctor in Visual Arts Curriculum, University of Tasmania
Launceston, Tasmania, 7250 Australia
pduncum@utas.edu.au

Michael J. Emme
Associate Professor of Art Education
University of Alberta, Department of Elementary Education
551 Education South, Edmonton, Alberta T6G 2G5 Canada

Lisette Ewing
Consultant/Teacher for Blind and Visually Impaired
4J School District–ESS Lane Regional Program
200 North Monroe, Eugene, OR 97402
doczwing@aol.com

Dennis Earl Fehr
Associate Professor of Art Education
Texas Tech University
P.O. Box 42081, Lubbock, TX 79409-2081
dfehr@ttv.edu

Kris Fehr
3616 60th Street, Lubbock, TX 79413
mamakkf@aol.com

Yvonne Gaudelius
Assistant Professor of Art Education and Women's Studies
The Pennsylvania State University
207 Arts Cottage, University Park, PA 16802
ymg100@psu.edu

Olivia Gude
Associate Professor and Coordinator of Art Education
University of Illinois–Chicago, 106 Jefferson Hall
929 West Harrison Street, Chicago, IL 60607-7038
gude@uic.edu

Karen Keifer-Boyd
Assistant Professor of Art Education
Texas Tech University
P.O. Box 42081, Lubbock, TX 79409-2081
KarenKB@ttu.edu

Laurel Lampela
Associate Professor, Cleveland State University
2307 Chester Avenue, Cleveland, OH 44118
l.lampela@csuohio.edu

Christine Ballengee Morris
Assistant Professor of Art Education
The Ohio State University
1179 University Drive, Newark, OH 43055
cmorris@pop.service.ohio-state.edu

Frank Pio
President, Turtle Island Center for the Arts
9 Woodlawn Avenue
Port Credit, Toronto, Ontario L5G 3K4, Canada
f.pio@utoronto.ca

Deborah Smith-Shank
Associate Professor of Art Education
Northern Illinois University, DeKalb, IL 60115-2883
debatart@niu.edu

Marianne Stevens Suggs
Professor of Art, Appalachian State University
Art Department, Wey Hall, Boone, NC 28607
suggsms@appstate.edu

Gayle Marie Weitz
Associate Professor of Art
Appalachian State University
Art Department, Wey Hall, Boone, NC 28607
weitzgm@am.appstate.edu

Mary Wyrick
Associate Professor, Buffalo State University
Art Education BI 102
1300 Elmwood Avenue, Buffalo, NY 14222-1115
wyrickml@snybufaa.cs.snybuf.edu

Index